HARMFUL SOCIETIES

Studies in Social Harm

Environmental harm: An eco-justice perspective
by Rob White (2013)

Harmful societies: Understanding social harm
by Simon Pemberton (2015)

New perspectives on Islamophobia and social harm
by Chris Allen (2016)

A sociology of harm
by Lynne Copson (2016)

Labour exploitation and work-based harm
by Sam Scott (2016)

Pharmaceuticals and social harm
by Sarah Payne (2017)

Global kitchens and super highways: Social harm and the political economy of food by Reece Walters (2017)

For further details see **www.policypress.co.uk**

HARMFUL SOCIETIES
Understanding social harm

Simon Pemberton

First published in Great Britain in 2015 by

Policy Press
University of Bristol
1–9 Old Park Hill
Bristol BS2 8BB
UK
+44 (0)117 331 4054
tpp-info@bristol.ac.uk
www.policypress.co.uk

North America office:
Policy Press
c/o The University of Chicago Press
1427 East 60th Street
Chicago, IL 60637, USA
t: +1 773 702 7700
f: +1 773 702 9756
sales@press.uchicago.edu
www.press.uchicago.edu

British Library Cataloguing in Publication Data
A catalogue record for this book is available from the British Library.

Library of Congress Cataloging-in-Publication Data
A catalog record for this book has been requested.

ISBN: 978 1 84742 794 6 (hardcover)

Cover design by Policy Press
Front cover image supplied by iStock
Printed and bound in Great Britain by CPI Group (UK) Ltd,
Croydon, CR0 4YY
Policy Press uses environmentally responsible print partners

Contents

List of tables and figures

Tables

Figures

List of abbreviations

Au	Australia
Aus	Austria
Be	Belgium
Ca	Canada
Ch	Chile
Cz	Czech Republic
De	Denmark
Es	Estonia
Fi	Finland
Fr	France
Ge	Germany
Gr	Greece
Hu	Hungary
Ir	Ireland
It	Italy
Ja	Japan
Ko	Republic of Korea
Me	Mexico
Nl	Netherlands
No	Norway
NZ	New Zealand
Po	Portugal
Pol	Poland
Ru	Russian Federation
Sl	Slovenia
SLR	Slovak Republic
Sp	Spain
Sw	Sweden
Tu	Turkey
UK	United Kingdom
US	United States of America

About the author

Simon Pemberton is a Birmingham Fellow jointly appointed to the Schools of Social Policy and Law at University of Birmingham, UK. He has researched and published widely in the areas of corporate and state harm, poverty and inequality, crime, social harm and criminalisation.

Acknowledgements

I have imagined this book for a long time, yet much of the thinking and analysis that has contributed to its ultimate conception owes a great deal to much valued friends and colleagues: Dave Gordon, Clare Hill, Paddy Hillyard, Christina Pantazis, Joe Sim, Eldin Fahmy, Dave Whyte, Karen Rowlingson and Stuart Connor. I am particularly grateful to Steve Tombs, for his detailed and thoughtful engagement with the typescript, which radically improved the initial draft, and to Policy Press, particularly Alison Shaw, for demonstrating considerable patience and an equal measure of faith when successive deadlines were not met. The analyses contained in this book owe a great deal to the patience and support of Sara Brookes. The usual disclaimers apply, of course. Sara, Finley and Freddy were the perfect inspiration to finish this project, and it could not have been done without their support and love.

Foreword

Each year and worldwide, millions of adults and children are killed or experience death, and many more are hurt or injured, from causes that are entirely preventable. For example, the most recent estimates reveal that close to 7 million children under 5 years of age died from diseases such as pneumonia, diarrhoea and malaria or due to pre-birth or intrapartum complications;[1] 1.2 million people died on the world's roads;[2] there were almost half a million deaths as a result of intentional homicide across the world;[3] and there were 378,000 global war deaths annually between 1985 and 1994.[4]

The general tendency of academic researchers has been to address the nature and causes of such harms, and their remedies, from within distinct and separate disciplines – primarily, social epidemiology, social policy, criminology and development studies. The nature of academic disciplinary boundaries is such that interdisciplinary, and multidisciplinary, approaches are rarely applied to the analyses of such harms.

The social harm approach, with its recent origins in the publication *Beyond criminology: Taking harm seriously*, by Paddy Hillyard and others in 2004,[5] sought to remedy this academic lacuna. Written as a critique of criminology, the authors sought to problematise the basis on which a distinct number of harms came to be seen as crimes and dealt with through an expensive, ineffective and ultimately socially harmful criminal justice system. At the same time they drew attention to other (potentially more harmful) events and situations that failed to attract the crime label, and therefore, the same level of social opprobrium. Their response was to call for a new social harm approach (or zemiological approach, taken from the Greek word *zemia*, meaning harm) which would encompass a typology of

---

[1] UN Inter-agency Group for Child Mortality Estimation (2012) *Levels and trends in child mortality: Report 2012*, New York: UNICEF.

[2] World Health Organization (2013) *Global status report on road safety 2013: Supporting a decade of action*, Geneva: WHO.

[3] UNODC (2013) *Global study on homicide 2013: Trends/contexts/data*, Vienna: United National Office on Drugs and Crime.

[4] Obermeyr, Z., Murray, C. and Gakidou, E. (2008) 'Fifty years of violent war deaths from Vietnam to Bosnia: analysis of data from the world health survey programme', *British Medical Journal*, vol 336, no 7659, pp 1482-86.

[5] Hillyard, P., Pantazis, C., Tombs, S. and Gordon, D. (2004) *Beyond criminology: Taking harm seriously*, London: Pluto Press.

social harms, irrespective of legal categorisation, and which could be responded to through progressive and democratic social policies.

The book series Studies in Social Harm seeks to offer a contribution to the disciplinary agenda of zemiology by encouraging fresh thinking on the nature of, and responses to, serious harms afflicting individuals and communities, both nationally and globally. It aims to provide intellectual (both in terms of theoretical and empirical) coherence to the study of social harms, drawing on interdisciplinary and multidisciplinary and different and innovative methodological approaches. Ultimately the book series aims to enhance knowledge on how social harms are mediated through social structures such as class, race, and gender, and are underpinned through different modes of social organisation.

Harmful societies by Simon Pemberton (Studies in Social Harm co-editor) is the second book in the series. Pemberton's book seeks to understand the 'harmful nature of contemporary capitalist societies' (p 9). Specifically, he attempts to unravel the ways in which varieties of capitalist formations – to a greater or lesser degree – jeopardise 'human flourishing'. Pemberton's book breaks new ground for the zemiological project in at least three distinct ways.

The first is in terms of the definition of social harm, which has thus far suffered from both ambiguity and confusion, and has resulted in a lack of consensus about its meaning. Pemberton's adoption of a 'human flourishing' approach, based on the theories of Doyal and Gough,[6,7] provides a much-needed ontological approach. Accordingly, individuals are said to experience harm, in terms of their physical and mental wellbeing, when they lack autonomy or when their social relationships are undermined.

The second is in relation to his unique typology of 'harm reduction regimes' (neoliberal, liberal, post-socialist corporatist, southern corporatist, meso-corporatist, northern corporatist and social democratic), which allows him to classify 31 countries according to five identifiable characteristics of harm reduction: mode of capitalist production, welfare provision, criminal justice system, regulatory system and role of social solidarity. The purpose of this exercise is to hypothesise (and eventually demonstrate) that, although the drive for surplus value, exploitation, alienation and the commodification

---

[6] Doyal, L. and Gough, I. (1982) 'A theory of human needs', *Critical Social Policy*, vol 4, no 10, pp 5-38.

[7] Doyal, L. and Gough, I. (1991) *A theory of human need*, Basingstoke: Palgrave Macmillan

of labour means that all capitalist societies are by their very nature harmful, the patterning of social harm is dependent on the specific nature of capitalist formation. For Pemberton, harm production can be understood in terms of a continuum with neoliberal regimes having the most destructive levels and forms of harm.

These theoretical and methodological underpinnings facilitate the third innovative aspect of his study; that is, the impressive collection of carefully chosen social indicators that facilitates the exploration of statistical associations between harms and harm reduction regime type for a selected number of countries. Pemberton's empirical mapping exercise provides evidence for his argument that the harms of capitalism are not uniform; some capitalist societies (generally those more neoliberal societies) have more harm, others less (often those exhibiting more social democratic tendencies). Thus, some varieties of capitalist formation through their welfare system, nature of criminal justice system, the role of social solidarity and so on, are better placed than others at ensuring that the harms endemic to capitalism are prevented.

As Pemberton accepts, the arguments developed and the evidence amassed for *Harmful societies* make depressing reading. Yet, it is arguably through these that an understanding of what a 'harm-free society' might look like emerges. This is a society that aims for human flourishing through ensuring people's physical and mental integrity, a level of autonomy and a sense of connectedness with others. In the context of the pressing need to develop utopian perspectives of alternative societies, Pemberton's book provides a unique contribution towards those imaginative states.

Christina Pantazis
Co-editor, Studies in Social Harm
School for Policy Studies, University of Bristol

ONE

Introduction

> When one individual inflicts bodily injury upon another, such injury that death results, we call the deed manslaughter; when the assailant knew in advance that the injury would be fatal, we call this deed murder. But when society places hundreds of proletarians in such a position that they inevitably meet a too early and an unnatural death ... when it deprives thousands of the necessaries of life, places them under conditions in which they cannot live ... forces them, through the strong arm of the law, to remain in such conditions until that death ensues which is the inevitable consequence – knows that these thousands of victims must perish, to remain in such conditions, its deed is murder just as surely as the deed of the single individual ... which seem what it is, because no man sees the murderer, because the death of the victim seems a natural one, since the offence is more one of omission than of commission. (Engels, 1845/1987, p 127)

So many of the sentiments conveyed through Engels' analysis in *The condition of the working class in England* (1845/1987) resonate with the themes of this book. For me, the analysis presented by Engels is one of the original, if not *the* original, social harm analysis. Engels not only described in forensic detail the harms visited on the proletariat in the Great Towns as they underwent immense social and economic transformation during the Industrial Revolution, but crucially he understood these harms as entirely preventable, a product of social relations that could be organised very differently to meet the needs of the many and not just the few. Engels correctly identified the disease, squalor and deprivation endured at this point in time, not to be 'natural', but an 'inevitable consequence' of the laissez-faire mode of capitalism that dominated 19th-century England. While critical scholars have sporadically engaged with such issues over time – particularly through the notions of structural violence and social injury – this form of analysis over the last 30 years has arguably been marginalised within the social sciences, giving way in many instances to individualised accounts of harm. In the wake of the latest episode of capitalist crisis and the resulting austerity policies put in place in many nation states, engaging with the questions that prompted Engels all those years ago in relation to laissez-faire capitalism are crucial if we are to document and explain harm production in the age of neoliberalism.

A starting point for this monograph, then, is the omission within contemporary social sciences of the forms of analysis that can answer the 'bigger' questions. In part, such analyses of structural harm have become 'academically unfashionable' with the rise of post-modernist/ post-structuralist accounts that favour more 'localised' narratives of harm, as well as 'politically unfashionable' in the context of the current 'neoliberal' hegemony. Thus, structural accounts of harm within the social sciences have recently come to be undermined by 'biographies of risk navigation', 'behavioural explanations' or 'narratives of individual resilience' that overstate the role of agency in the experience of harm. In addition, the increasing specialisation within academia means the social sciences have tended to promote fragmented approaches to harm, with disciplines and sub-disciplines interested in very specific forms of harm, and have, consequently, produced discrete forms of bounded knowledge. It is for these reasons that critical social scientists have begun to explore the potential of the social harm approach as a means to hold an alternative lens to contemporary capitalist society, and in doing so, to promote more systematic and objective analyses of harm.

This book seeks to develop the social harm lens as a means to respond to liberal philosophies that have created a prevailing orthodoxy in relation to the production of harm in capitalist societies. This orthodoxy serves to foreground individual agency within discourses of harm, so that our shared understanding of harmful events tends towards explanations couched in the biological traits, personality characteristics or behaviours of those involved. Thus, there are well established liberal philosophical and legal theories that articulate elaborate and complex theories of individual responsibility that explain aetiologies of interpersonal harms, or that serve to cast 'blame' on those who experience injury or loss due to socioeconomic harms, such as unemployment, poverty or workplace accidents. However, the social contexts that determine individual-level harms (such as suicide or homicide), as well as the harmful aspects of social structures, are less well understood. The analysis presented in the remainder of the book seeks to challenge three aspects of the liberal orthodoxy to harm.

First, harm in liberal discourses tends to be constructed through notions of negative liberty, which restrict our understanding of injury and loss to coercive interventions that interfere with the pursuit of individual freedoms. In contrast, a social harm approach, predicated on notions of positive liberty, is able to capture harms that result when human flourishing is compromised by the denial of social resources necessary to enable the exercise of life choices. Second, liberal discourses tend to restrict the focus of harms to the individual, which neglects the socially situated nature of agents, abstracting them from the relationships they are located in and through which they are constituted. This has a significant impact on analyses of harm – serving to deny that the harms individuals experience arise from wider relationships in which they are embedded, as well as failing to capture the consequential or secondary harms that result beyond the original individual harmed to have an impact on other connected individuals and communities. Finally, the abstracted rational actor, as the primary unit of harm analysis, fails to capture how analogous acts may be experienced as more or less harmful by different social groups. Thus, depending on the resources and social capital we are able to draw on, our ability to respond to specific harms can differ significantly, which in turn means that harms can have contrasting impacts on a person's life chances.

The point is that these orthodoxies have served to distort societal understanding of harm production. The fact that, for example, in the UK annually, over 18,000 (England and Wales) (ONS, 2014) people die as a result of excess winter deaths, 29,000 lives are ended prematurely from air pollution (COMEAP, 2010) and another 13,000 people die (Great Britain) from occupational lung disease and cancers (HSE, 2014) – tend to be explained away as either the course of 'natural' events or the 'by-products' of social progress from which we all benefit. If we are to debunk these orthodoxies, we require a sociological 'lens' that can capture the mass production of capitalist harm and that then locates these processes within the very fabric of our societies. The concept of social harm, then, is proposed as being ideally placed to provide such a lens, but as many readers might be asking, what is social harm? And where did it come from?

Origins of 'social harm': the story so far...

This section provides a schematic view of the development of social harm as a concept. It is not the intention that the book will dwell on the minutiae of this story, however; rather, it is important for our purposes that some aspects are understood in order to contextualise contemporary debates in relation to social harm. Those on the margins of criminology's disciplinary boundaries have long discussed the possibility of extending the notion of crime to incorporate broader harms, particularly the harms caused by corporations and state bodies that had hitherto fallen outside the boundaries of criminological study. These discussions originate from debates had within criminology during the 1930s and 1940s (Sutherland, 1940, 1945; Tappan, 1947). Crucially, Sutherland began to use the notion of 'social injury' to extend the definition of crime to include the injurious activities of corporations within his ground-breaking studies of white-collar and corporate crime (Sutherland, 1945, p 132). Twenty-five years passed until the Schwendingers' seminal work on state crime (1970) (who were influenced as students by Sutherland's work; Schwendinger and Schwendinger, 2001), when they deployed the notion of 'social injury' as a tool to incorporate structural harms such as racism, poverty and homelessness into their analyses of crime. This work proved to be hugely influential on a generation of North American critical criminologists who followed, using the notion of social harm to define the parameters of their criminological inquiries (Kramer, 1985; Michalowski, 1985; Tifft, 1995).

However, it was not until the late 1990s that concerted efforts to systematically develop the notion of social harm took place. These began with a number of academic discussions at the annual conferences of the European Group for the Study of Deviance and Social Control, in particular in Spezies and Palanga, and a conference dedicated to the possibilities offered by a social harm approach in Dartington in 1999. These discussions most tangibly resulted in the publication of *Beyond criminology* (Hillyard et al, 2004). While this edited collection represented a broad range of positions, the contributions were unified by the perceived deficiencies of the concept of crime as a lens to capture the full range of harms that impact on our lives. These deficiencies stem from the fact that crime encompasses many petty events while it excludes a multitude of serious harms, a significant reason for this being the individualistic notion of intent on which crime is based, which consequently fails to capture the most significant causes of avoidable harm that result from inactivity and moral indifference. Thus, excluded from criminological analyses have been some of the mass harms caused by corporate or state bodies, and most significantly from the social harm perspective, this lens has failed to adequately capture structural harms. For the contributors to *Beyond criminology*, the desire to develop objective and systematic analyses of harm were prompted by key political concerns, that specifically related to the rise of neoliberalism and the socioeconomic restructuring set in motion since the late 1970s. Thus, the analyses in *Beyond criminology*

–

sought to begin the task of documenting the harms generated by a shift away from the social democratic institutions of the post-war period to neoliberal forms of social organisation championed by the 'Washington Consensus'. Harms that have resulted from both the retrenchment of the social state, through the 'rolling back' of welfare and regulatory systems, alongside the expansion of the coercive or strong state, through the increasing criminalisation of social life and the corollary use of prison, as mechanisms to deal with the problems created by market forces.

It would be misleading to present *Beyond criminology* as an entirely coherent project, however. Indeed, a variety of positions were assumed, with some authors proposing the abandonment of criminology for an alternative field of study, while others sought to develop the notion of crime to incorporate broader social harms – thus furthering and extending existing scholarly projects within the field of critical criminology (see, for example, Ward, 2004). For critics of *Beyond criminology*, the social harm critique presented a caricature of criminology that failed to acknowledge the contributions of 'critical criminology' or 'sociological criminologists', and in reality, the much-needed reformulation of the notion of crime to include wider social harms or 'deepenings' in criminological knowledge have been part of the disciplinary enterprise for some time (Muncie, 2005, p 200; Hughes, 2006). Indeed, for some within criminology, there was a sense that *Beyond criminology* represented the 'emperor's new clothes'. But for many others, the publication of *Beyond criminology* and *Criminal obsessions* (Hillyard et al, 2004; Dorling et al, 2008) posed important questions of criminology, leading them to draw on social harm to frame new criminological analyses. This facilitated, or at the very least, broadened, the notion of crime to deal with hitherto unexplored phenomena, such as the structural harms of globalisation (Cain and Howe, 2008; Ezeonu, 2008; Michalowski, 2011), technological harms (McGuire, 2007; Hope, 2013), natural 'disasters' (Faust and Kauzlarich, 2008), or the harms resulting from the criminalisation of 'suspect communities' (Doody, 2010).

In contrast, *Beyond criminology* marked a point for some critical scholars (including myself), to move beyond the disciplinary confines of criminology, as well as the criminal justice system, to seek an alternative 'space' through which to develop systematic analyses and progressive responses to harm. The debates over whether one could coherently stretch the concept of crime to encompass a host of practices and events appeared to be exhausted, and the resolution of such discussions did not appear to meaningfully progress the social harm debate. For these writers, if the social harm debate remained within the confines of criminology, it would be stuck within a conceptual cul-de-sac, whereby the individualising tendencies of the criminal law would constrain the possibility of producing systematic and holistic analyses of harm. *Beyond criminology* most significantly had brought together not only critical criminologists to bemoan the failings of criminology, but drew together academics with different social science backgrounds who arguably provided some of the most interesting and challenging contributions to the collection. This gave impetus to the notion that an alternative academic space did indeed exist 'beyond criminology', where more productive and rounded analyses of harms could be located. Moreover, through these discussions it was obvious that many of the concerns voiced in relation to criminology actually transcended the discipline. In fact, a wider malaise within the social sciences could be detected within current academic trends. Thus the dominance of the 'risk society' thesis within social theory, or the underclass thesis within poverty discourses, prompted a number of analyses that serve to individualise the allocation of harms within society. It is intended that this monograph will contribute to the task of establishing an academic space, whereby the vicissitudes of life in capitalist society may be more accurately detailed.

Outlining the parameters of a social harm

Detailing the failings of a discipline or disciplines is perhaps an easier task than resolving the issues identified through this critique. Indeed, if social harm is to be more than a critique of criminology or an 'oppositional' discourse, and is to exist as a field of study in its own right, then a series of difficult issues relating to the definition of social harm and how it is measured must be resolved. The point is that this book does not purport to offer a definitive approach to these issues; rather, it is hoped that it will provide a schema that can be developed or contested, to inform future social harm analyses.

The existing literature confusingly makes reference to both social harm and zemiology, and at times these terms have been used interchangeably. For some, including myself, social harm represents the study of socially mediated harms, whereas zemiology, derived from the Greek *xemia* for harm, denotes the study of harm. As a field of study, whether the label of social harm or zemiology is adopted is an important question, and arguably one that is more than an issue of semantics. Zemiology is preferable, insofar as a by-product of *Beyond criminology* has been the cooption of the language of social harm into criminological discourse; in addition, the term is used within health discourses to denote broader harms related to addiction. Thus, zemiology would serve to demarcate those critical scholars whose interest lies 'beyond criminology' from criminologists using the notion of social harm, to establish an alternative field of study. Social harm therefore becomes the organising concept for zemiology as a field of study. When these distinctions are drawn, the emergent characteristics of zemiology can be more clearly articulated as distinct from other fields, in particular, criminology. It follows, then, that if zemiology is to be viewed as a distinct perspective or field of study, it must have distinguishing features that demarcate the knowledge(s) it produces from existing disciplinary approaches. Having said this, it is probably a little premature to claim that a new field of study exists, although hopefully this work contributes with others to its establishment; but with this in mind, it is appropriate that the term 'social harm' is deployed for the remainder of the book.

For those working with the notion of social harm, and particularly potential zemiologists, some key features emerge from the literature to date that give a greater sense of what a future field of study might look like. The remainder of this section seeks to summarise these characteristics and to demonstrate how these will, in turn, inform the organising themes of the book.

First, as already alluded to, the concept of 'social harm' seeks to provide an alternative 'lens' that captures the vicissitudes of contemporary life. Principally, the approach seeks to develop conceptual and methodological tools that more accurately map the harms that occur within capitalist societies. Thus, the social harm 'lens' is consciously detached and develops independently of dominant liberal discourses that promote myopic approaches to harm. It is proposed here that the emergent field of study, zemiology, offers a less restricted disciplinary space to develop such a 'lens'. Thus, 'zemiologists' might engage with more productive definitional discussions than currently undertaken within, for example, criminology or law, to produce a 'lens' that more accurately captures the many injurious ways that human flourishing is compromised in capitalist societies (Hillyard and Tombs, 2004).

Second, the 'harms' many of us tend to concern ourselves with are, at best, rare occurrences, or have insignificant impacts on our life chances. It is often the case that the harms that dominate the political debates and media portrayals of contemporary life are those associated with individual-level harms, such as crime and anti-social behaviour, the harms perpetuated by the relatively powerless and marginalised.

Yet, as this book seeks to demonstrate, the injury caused by state bodies and corporations, as well as the very organisation of our societies, can cause a higher incidence of serious harms (Hillyard and Tombs, 2004).

Third, the underpinning logic of capitalist societies serves to prioritise interpersonal harms over organisational and structural harms. This is based on the distinction drawn between intentional and non-intentional acts, with the former viewed as being more worthy of moral opprobrium. In some instances this hierarchy serves to shape social scientists' analyses of harm – in particular, criminologists have traditionally focused on harms resulting from intentional acts. This distinction appears to be difficult to sustain, if it results in partial analyses of harm that exclude the more serious structural harms. Indeed, if systematic and objective analyses of harm are to be developed, alternative approaches to responsibility are required to acknowledge that the harms that cause the most widespread social injury are not caused by intentional acts, but rather, result from the omission to act or societal indifference to suffering (Pemberton, 2004b).

Fourth, the focus of social harm analyses are not predicated on the question of whether or not harm was intended, but whether harms can be considered to be preventable. Thus, the notion that structural harms are somehow 'natural' features of a given society is actively contested. Rather, such harms are viewed as a direct consequence of prevailing political, economic and policy decisions. These decisions shape the very forms that our societies take, and consequently, the harms produced by these social arrangements. The examination of different forms of capitalist society in this book will demonstrate how the nature and extent of harm varies between societies depending on their formation. Indeed, the fact that some societies have lower incidences of harm than others would suggest that harm is not inevitable, but rather a product of the way we choose to organise the societies in which we live.

Fifth, the purpose to social harm analyses is not only to better understand the harmful organisation of our societies, but to contribute to political and policy debates that have the potential to reform these injurious arrangements. Indeed, it is hoped that by demonstrating the variance in capitalist harms, that it comes to be acknowledged that even within the ideological parameters fixed by globalisation and global capital, less harmful forms of capitalism than the neoliberal form are, indeed, possible.

Outline of the book

The principal empirical focus of the book is to understand the harmful nature of contemporary capitalist societies. In so doing the book seeks to capture the variance between societies in the extent of these harms, and to understand how similarly placed societies are able to 'design out' specific harms, while others do not. It is important to make three caveats in relation to the analytical focus on capitalism. First, this is not to say that other forms of social organisation, such as communism, feudalism or theocracies, do not cause harms or are necessarily less harmful forms. The organising features of these societies clearly differ from capitalism and merit similar forms of investigation, yet, on a global scale, capitalism as a mode of organisation is, albeit with a few notable exceptions, the 'only show in town', and for this reason, demands our immediate attention. Second, the focus on capitalist harm does not seek to downplay the harms of patriarchy or neocolonialism that occur within these societies, and nor should we ignore the intersectionality of class with relations of gender, ethnicity and sexuality that determine a host of social harms. These are complex issues that probably could not be dealt with adequately in several volumes, let alone one book. Third, capitalism produces resilient and often dynamic systems that produce goods and services that benefit large swathes of these populations – this is not disputed here. However, what the book does seek to question are the injuries that result from this form of social organisation, and what can be done to remedy the harmful organisation of our societies.

The remainder of the book is divided into five chapters. Chapter Two principally details the social harm lens to be used in the analyses provided in later chapters. In doing so, the chapter reviews existing approaches and definitions of social harm in order to develop this lens. It is perhaps unsurprising, given the disparate nature of this literature, that the concept remains ambiguous and somewhat amorphous in nature. The task here is to outline the boundaries as well as the content of the concept, and to develop devices that determine whether particular social events fall within its parameters or not. In doing so, the chapter seeks to outline both the 'social' and the 'harm' in the definition of social harm. In respect of the latter, an ontological approach is advocated that identifies harms as specific events or instances where 'human flourishing' is demonstrably compromised. It is proposed that harms can be categorised in the following ways: physical/mental health harms; autonomy harms; and relational harms. In terms of the 'social', 'socially mediated' harms are viewed as 'preventable harms' insofar as they are either 'foreseeable' events or the result of 'alterable' social conditions. The remainder of the book then focuses on the extent to which harm may be considered 'preventable' insofar as the variance in harms experienced between different nation states is suggestive of the fact that they result from 'alterable' social conditions.

Chapter Three develops this theme, that harms are not inevitable but are determined by the forms of organisation our societies take. Thus it introduces the notion of capitalist harm – harms that are inherent to the capitalist form of organisation. It is argued that the form harms take in capitalist societies will be similar in nature; however, as capitalist formations have followed different developmental trajectories, resulting in contrasting forms of organisation, it logically follows that the experience and extent of harms will not be uniform. Thus, the extent of harm experienced will be patterned according to the particular features of societies. The chapter proposes a typology of harm reduction regimes, which group nation states according to the harm reduction/production features they demonstrate. In doing so, it outlines the methodological approach adopted, whereby specific features of the nation states included in the study are used to explain the variance in harms between different regime types.

Chapter Four examines the performance of the selected nation states and the regime types in relation to a number of physical harms: homicide, suicide, infant mortality, obesity and road traffic injuries. Perhaps with the exception of 'homicide', the other harms in this chapter are most commonly viewed as the result of the 'lottery of life', often explained away as the result of individual biology. The chapter reveals the features of societies that serve to protect against these harms – in particular, the extent to which different societies disrupt, as a result of welfare systems, regulation or broader social relations, the impulses of capitalism to commodify human life.

Similarly Chapter Five scrutinises the performance of the selected nation states and the regime types in relation to autonomy and relational harms. The harms included in this chapter are poverty, child poverty, financial insecurity, long working hours, youth unemployment and social isolation. In contrast to the physical harms discussed in the previous chapter, these harms are not necessarily immediately obvious, and therefore space is devoted to outlining the ways in which these conditions injuriously compromise human flourishing. The chapter demonstrates the facets of specific societies that appear to militate against or serve to exacerbate the production of these harms – in particular, the extent to which societies fetter the extraction of surplus value, therefore willing to regulate the capital–labour relation and provide support for those who are excluded from paid work.

Chapter Six draws on the analysis presented in Chapters Four and Five to provide an overview of how the regimes perform in relation to the harms presented in the study. From this discussion, the chapter presents regimes as a sliding scale, from the most harmful forms to the least harmful. In doing so, it examines the features of nation states that appear to make them more or less harmful, and serves to explain the variance in the experience and extent of harm.

Ultimately, much has been written about the potential of the social harm approach, and I do not doubt its potential, yet at the moment, it remains a relatively empty space, insofar as few studies have actually sought to develop the conceptual 'lens' and to operationalise it through empirical study. It is hoped that this book will contribute to how we may begin to collectively imagine an alternative approach to the study of harm.

TWO

Defining social harm

This chapter outlines the social harm 'lens' used in this book. Although the obvious point to start this task is with the existing literature on the topic, while this offers important pointers, it is disparate and fragmented in nature, and the concept of social harm that emerges is vague and ambiguous. A principal aim of this chapter, therefore, is to consolidate this work into a single historical account, and to garner a number of insights from this literature to assist with the development of the social harm lens.

Importantly, from this discussion, two dilemmas are identified in relation to establishing 'social harm' as an alternative lens. First, to provide the concept of social harm with a form that ensures it is distinct from other concepts, this requires conceptual boundaries that demarcate the phenomena that it exists to investigate. If these parameters are highly prescriptive, there is a possibility that the lens the concept offers is foreclosed and consequently fails to capture the full range of harms advocated by the approach. Yet if the conceptual boundaries remain too open, there is also the possibility that the concept becomes a 'catch-all', encompassing a host of activities that we might dislike or disapprove, yet are not necessarily harmful. Second, as the previous chapter argued, a more accurate 'lens' for the study of social harms is only possible if the concept is detached from dominant liberal frames. Thus, social harm as a concept must be located outside of the prevailing discourses of harm. However, in this process of detachment, locating the concept on the 'outside' of these discourses could lead to accusations that social harm is a 'subjective' notion, as it is not imbued with the legitimacy of dominant frames for which shared societal understanding exists. As suggested later in the chapter, this argument does not necessarily defeat the case for conceptual 'detachment', and neither should the social harm approach advocate a 'value-free' position as a means of compensation; it is important that the values that inform the constitution of the 'alternative lens' are laid bare, so that the empirical claims that are generated from it are open to critical scrutiny.

Historical development of the social harm approach

A key challenge for those wishing to establish zemiology as a distinct field of study is the absence of an established definition of social harm, and so a clear starting point is to map the sporadic and somewhat disparate existing literature to develop the organising concept. With few exceptions this literature has developed on the margins of criminology, where social harm is used as a means to expand the notion of crime. Obviously, this book seeks to develop a definition of social harm as an organising concept for zemiology, a distinct field of study to that of criminology. Disregarding the attempts to extend the notion of crime, this literature offers an important departure point from which the concept of social harm may be developed. As suggested, the chapter reviews the existing literature, identifying four principle approaches to defining social harm: social injury; sociological categories; ontological; and democratic. The point to this typology is to impose some order on the fairly chaotic evolution of the notion of social harm. However, it is not intended that the historical genesis of social harm is, in anyway, presented as a cohesive picture. Moreover, there is a tendency within the criminological literature to use the term without explicit reference to a definition. It is also important to note that the literature relating to 'criminal harm' is not included here (see, for example, Greenfield and Paoli, 2013), as it represents a distinct criminological enterprise to remedy the neglect of 'harm' within discussions of 'crime'.

The point is, there appears to be significant disconnect between the uses of the term 'social harm', with little reference to previous work, and the literature lacks cohesion and coherence in places. In fact, what emerges from this 'potted history' is the fact that few definitions of social harm actually exist. The role of this chapter is to review existing definitions, and to draw together the strands of existing approaches. Emergent properties can be found within this work that offer clues to the possible tenets of a fully-fledged concept of social harm. This section discusses each approach to defining social harm in turn, examining the relative merits and weaknesses, as well as identifying themes to be developed in the eventual definition used in this book.

Social injury approaches

Given the historical roots of social harm in criminology, it is unsurprising that initial attempts to define the notion drew on legal categories. For many, Sutherland's (1945) attempts to broaden the notion of crime to encompass the injury caused by white-collar activities signal the awakening of criminological curiosity in relation to social harm. Sutherland (1945, p 132) sought to reframe criminological inquiry by arguing that activities that are labelled criminal should cause tangible 'social injury' and attract 'legal sanction'. Sutherland used the notion of 'social injury' to broaden criminology's horizons to encompass a range of white-collar harms that existed in the quasi-criminal realm of administrative and civil law, that he perceived to be cognate to traditional criminal harms. In many respects, Sutherland's work does not represent a significant break with criminological tradition; however, it provided a platform for others to consider alternative and more imaginative approaches to harm. In a foreword to the reprint of their classic article, 'Defenders of order or guardians of human rights', the Schwendingers (2001) note the influence of Sutherland's work on social injury alongside the political events of the 1970s, which inspired them to consider a broader approach to harm than the one offered by criminology at that point. For the Schwendingers, criminological study should focus on the social injury that results from the violation of basic human rights. By drawing on 'basic rights', the Schwendingers were able to label a range of structural harms, such as racism, imperialism, sexism and poverty, as criminal.

Through rejecting 'legalistic' definitions of crime, the Schwendingers developed an explicitly value-oriented definition of criminal harm. This attracted similar criticisms to those expressed by Tappan in relation to Sutherland's work. For example, Cohen (1993) describes the Schwendingers' expansive use of human rights to define starvation and poverty (1970) as state crimes as a 'moral crusade'. The question of values and objectivity in relation to the definition of social harm becomes a recurrent theme to which we return at various points in this chapter. Yet the human rights approach should not be rejected on these grounds. More problematic is the constitution of human rights. To begin with, human rights heavily reflect liberal democratic values and individualist reasoning. Moreover, as rights are won through political struggle, they represent the interests of a number of social groups and, consequently, are contradictory by their very nature. Therefore, there are too many tensions inherent within a human rights framework to make it a useful normative base for social harm. A conceptual 'step back' is required before human rights may be used by social harm. However, this is not to dispute the utility of rights in constructing political claims to have harmful events acknowledged and remedied.

The Schwendingers do not make explicit reference to the notion of harm (1970, 2001), preferring to use Sutherland's notion of 'social injury', a term that remains somewhat nebulous in nature in the works of these writers. Moreover, while much has been made of the contribution of the Schwendingers to the notion of social harm (1970), little space within the seminal article is devoted to explaining their rights-based approach. Yet this is perhaps not as important as it may initially seem. The Schwendingers, as Sutherland before them, inspired a generation of North American critical criminologists to frame their criminological inquiries through the notion of social harm (1970). Indeed, the works of Kramer (1985), Michalowski (1985) and Tifft and Sullivan (2001), influenced by the Schwendingers, are arguably pivotal in the establishment of the notion of social harm. While the social injury approach has returned to either existing legal systems or legal discourses to frame their definitions, this is not an approach pursued here – as suggested above, it delimits the potential scope of the social harm approach. However, as will become clear later, important themes emerge from this work that were not developed by the Schwendingers, but that recur in later definitions of social harm. First, by framing injury or harm as the violation of basic rights, we are compelled to understand that 'the abrogation of these rights ... limits the individual's chance to fulfil himself in many spheres of life' (Schwendinger and Schwendinger, 1975, p 137). Thus the 'conceptual step back' encouraged above means that we understand harm as an injurious event insofar as it impinges on the realisation of human potential. These concerns appear to demarcate many works that form the 'social harm' literature, in particular, ontological approaches that are addressed later. Second, the Schwendingers importantly argue that individual 'criminal' harms should be placed into the context of broader social relations, bemoaning criminology as being 'blind to the fact that extensive social planning makes it possible to evaluate, mitigate or eliminate the social conditions which generate criminal behaviour' (1970, p 135). Moreover, for the Schwendingers, these social structures are not only generative in nature, but aspects of these relations constitute harms, '... if the terms imperialism, racism, sexism, and poverty are abbreviated signs for theories of social relationships or social systems which cause the systematic abrogation of basic rights' (1975, p 137). Again, this identifies a theme that then runs through the social harm literature, seeking to understand the structural determinants of harm, or, to put it another way, that explicates the 'social' in 'social harm'.

Sociological categories

Acknowledging the problems associated with the social injury approach, and the ways that state-derived definitions of harm potentially limit the lens through which we view the vicissitudes of contemporary society, sociological definitions emerge to counter these shortcomings. Notable work from the 2000s takes a decisive step away from legal definitions of harm to draw on sociological concepts and methods (Muncie, 2000; Hillyard and Tombs, 2004). In doing so, the approach seeks to generate categories that are constituent elements of social harm. Undoubtedly, such approaches offer concepts of social harm that are potentially 'more theoretically coherent and imaginative, and more politically progressive approaches' (Hillyard and Tombs, 2004, p 19). However, by detaching from existing and recognised frameworks, such approaches are open to accusations of moral relativism.

In *Beyond criminology*, Hillyard and Tombs (2004) provide the most considered exemplar of the 'categories' approach to defining social harm, which has inspired a number of subsequent empirical analyses (Naughton, 2007; Doody, 2010). Hillyard and Tombs seek to develop a concept of harm that is able to 'encompass harms which are deleterious to people's welfare from the cradle to the grave' (2004, p 18). They suggest that such an approach would be constituted by the following categories of harm: physical, financial/economic, emotional/ psychological and cultural safety. For Hillyard and Tombs (2004, p 20), these categories are purposively open-ended, as the 'social harm approach is partially to be defined in its very operationalisation, in its efforts to measure social harms', which is critical to the development of this lens. Thus for Hillyard and Tombs (2004), the empirical applications of the concept forms part of the productive process of defining harm.

The attempt to generate categories of harm independent of traditional discursive frames is important, and these represent fundamental elements of the zemiological approach. Indeed, the principals established by Hillyard and Tombs (2004) specifically encourage the definition of harm to be an open-ended and ongoing process, that moves back and forth between conceptualisation to empirical measurement to refine the definition of social harm. Alone, however, open-ended categories are not sufficient guides to define the concept of harm (Pemberton, 2007; Pantazis and Pemberton, 2009; Yar, 2012). As Yar notes:

> … a lack of specificity leaves the concept lacking the very
> same ontological reality that is postulated as grounds for
> rejecting the concept of crime … nowhere in the writings is
> there a concerted attempt to give the concept any analytical
> specificity ie to define what makes something a "harm" or
> "harmful" or, what distinguishes the "harmful" from the
> non harmful? (Yar, 2012, p 59)

Yar (2012) raises an important issue in relation to the 'categories'
approach. While Hillyard and Tombs (2004) are correct that the
definition of social harm will evolve through empirical refinement,
there is something omitted from the equation, as Yar (2012) suggests,
that enables us to distinguish 'the harmful from the non harmful',
which, in all likelihood, remains a philosophical/conceptual question
rather than an empirical one. In other words, to be able to identify
harm through empirical study, we must first develop a rationale to
discern why specific instances of injury or loss are serious enough to
be considered harmful. Otherwise we are left with a version of social
harm that captures a host of grievances and is unable to distinguish
between serious harms and minor personal hardships.

Ontological approaches

Up to this point, it remains difficult to discern what 'social harm'
actually is. What is clear is the intention of those using the term
to develop a broader lens to study harm than are readily available.
However, through opening out the parameters of this lens without
a conceptual framework to provide an analytical focus, it becomes a
'catch-all' definition. Thus, it appears to lack the specificity necessary
to make it a meaningful concept. Yet, if we return to the work of the
Schwendingers (1970), we see the emergence of an important thematic
that offers a solution to the void identified. As noted earlier, the
Schwendingers, in their seminal work, touched on the idea that harm
may be identified through an understanding of human flourishing.
Thus, that harm may result when human potential is curtailed
through identifiable actions, practices or relations. In this vein, notable
definitions of social harm have emerged that seek to locate analyses of
harm within an ontological framework, by considering essentially the
events that compromise self-realisation.

A number of ontological frameworks have developed in order to
identify what the essential components of being are, so that when
these facets are compromised or absent from our lives, it can be said

that an individual experiences harm. One variety of this framework can be found in the human needs definition of social harm. This was first pioneered by Tifft and Sullivan (2001, p 191), who identify social harm as acts or conditions 'that interfere with the fulfilment of fundamental needs and obstruct the spontaneous unfolding of human potential.' It is a pity in some respects that this definition was used in order to develop theories of restorative justice, as little room is devoted to developing this notion of social harm. Consequently some important details are missed. In particular, it is unclear which human needs should constitute the definition of harm or, for that matter, how we should proceed in selecting such needs and the specific relationships to instances of harm. Following from this work, Pemberton (2004a, 2007) and Pantazis and Pemberton (2009) deployed Doyal and Gough's (1984, 1991) theory of human need to fill these gaps. According to this definition of harm, the non-fulfilment of specified needs leads to identifiable harms. Thus, by generating a list of needs adapted from the work of Doyal and Gough (1984, 1991), measures of harm were able to be developed.

Independently, and without reference to previous needs-based definitions, Majid Yar (2012) frames his definition of social harm within theories of recognition. Yar (2012, p 60) suggests that recognition offers both 'a theory of human needs and their violation'. In respect of the latter, Yar (2012, p 59) argues that recognition enables the determination 'at a fundamental anthropological level the basic needs that compromise the conditions of human integrity and wellbeing'. Accordingly, he claims it is possible to identify an order of human needs that constitute social harm: love, rights and esteem. Therefore, social harm is viewed as the 'intersubjective experience of being refused recognition with respect to any of these or all of these needs' (Yar, 2012, p 59). Yar's work correctly (2012) focuses our attention on the relational nature of harm, allowing us to consider the injuries of social isolation, as well as misrecognition as harm. Yet the needs Yar identifies are inevitably highly subjective in nature, so how emotional needs such as love and esteem are operationalised in empirical study become the 'technical issues', to which Hillyard and Tombs (2004) refer, for future social harm analyses to resolve.

Needs-based definitions of social harm have not been without criticism. Lasslett suggests that the needs-based approach adopted previously by the author 'suffers from a fatal error, namely it confuses harm with injustice' (2010, p 13), while Garside argues that it is a 'static conceptualisation, which implies that "human essence" and "human need" exist in a state logically prior to ... the social relationships into which humans enter' (2013, p 256). Instead, Lasslett (2010), drawing on the work of Lukacs, argues that 'the category, social harm, captures moments where the relations, processes and flows of social being either disrupt or fail to preserve the structures of organic and inorganic being' (p 13). Lasslett (2010) suggests that this Marxist ontological framework has three specific advantages. First, by 'delinking harm from norms', a field of study may develop that avoids 'Tappanian critiques' relating to the objectivity of our studies. Second, the unification of both the organic and social nature of being serves to focus social harm on the most serious harms, rather than focusing on acts that fail to have a significant impact on our lives. Finally, by grounding his definition in a 'triangular ontological totality' which forms the basis of human life, Lasslett argues that this avoids defining harm 'abstractly', so that harms are contextualised explicitly within the existing modes of production that determine them. Garside (2013), seeking to develop Lasslett's approach, draws on Meszaros (a student of Lukacs) to further articulate the notion of 'social metabolism', in other words, the interplay between the primary mediation (that humans guarantee their needs through a relationship with nature and each other) and second mediation (the forms that social organisations take to either realise human actualisation or to disrupt such flourishing). Garside continues '... under the antagonistic second order mediations of capital these fundamental human needs are systematically threatened and undermined. This is what scholars refer to when they write about the social harms of capitalism' (2013, p 263).

Both Lasslett and Garside's application of Marxist ontological theories to the definition of social harm make fundamental contributions – in particular, they advance the ways we explain and understand the specific relationships between the incidence of harm and to capitalist organisation. However, while these approaches eschew needs-based approach, it is not clear from either how we move from these important ontological yet abstract discussions to a more concrete empirical position. Yet, particularly in the case of Garside's use of Meszaros, this explicitly draws on the lexicon of need and notions of human fulfilment – as an aside, which specific needs are not discussed beyond basic physical needs. The point is that whatever way you cut it, whichever position you adopt in ontological terms, whether you are committed to the *a priori* human essence or one that is historically constituted – we require a device to empirically identify harms and needs however we conceive and wherever we situate them, ontologically speaking, seem as good a starting point as any.

Notwithstanding these schisms, the emerging ontological paradigm appears to offer a clearer sense of the 'social' in social harm. Hitherto, in the definitions discussed in this chapter, the notion of the social is either omitted altogether, or appears to be implicit in the descriptions of structures or contexts that perpetuate harm. It would appear for those using ontological definitions of social harm that there are distinct motivations behind the insistence on the 'social'. Thus, the 'social' is used to determine those harms that are 'socially mediated' (Pemberton, 2007) rather than those that originate from processes located in the natural world. The distinction between harms resulting from social and natural processes, however, is not necessarily clear-cut. The purpose of using the notion of 'socially mediated' harm is to allow social harm to frame analyses that capture social processes that intervene and interrupt the natural world in ways that are harmful. In so doing we can consider the ways in which human life is prematurely ended according to the standards of a given society, that otherwise may be considered 'natural events'. Yar (2012, p 63) offers some illumination on this matter:

> We must distinguish here those harms that are properly social, which emanate from the actions and inactions of humans (individually and collectively) from those harms that arise ultimately from natural facts and processes that lie beyond the capacity for human intervention.

The question of human intervention or the prevention of harm to which Yar makes reference is of paramount importance to the social harm approach. This is not necessarily a question for moral philosophy alone, but an empirical one as well, whereby the resources and means of a society may be evoked to understand whether intervention is possible.

Furthermore, these works have sought to develop the notion of the 'socially mediated' as a mechanism to capture the complexities of harm production in contemporary societies. In other words, to produce analyses that not only accurately describe harms, but also to be able to explain their production. Thus, in order to escape the individualised explanations of criminology, these definitions have sought to identify contexts as well as actions that cause harm. Lasslett offers the view that 'a discipline based on social harm would aim to approximate with greater clarity how these (capitalist) processes, flows and relations also produce particular forms of harm' (2010, p 11). Lasslett's (2010) definition points to the details of social organisation, such as the 'processes, flows and relations' that social harm should be attuned to. Perhaps where his discussion is less clear is how this definition would apply to alternative modes of social organisation – although he notes that historical studies should address this question. Moreover, while Lasslett's definition is not intended to reflect social relations of patriarchy, neocolonialism and so on, a social harm approach should be equipped to analyse all forms of harm. Therefore its lens should not be delimited by the way we frame the 'social'. Tifft and Sullivan offer a broader notion of the 'social' in social harm, which they suggest is denoted by 'social conditions, social arrangements, or actions of intent or indifference' (2001, p 191). This definition allows us to capture a range of relationships, not only the economic, but also comparative forms of study between capitalist and non-capitalist forms of organisation. Moreover, Tifft and Sullivan's (2001) definition allows social harm analyses to compare and contrast harms from different sources – social structures, organisations, as well as the interpersonal.

Ultimately, we could just choose the line that harms happen, that is the basis of our investigation. Then we would have a concept of harm, not social harm. The social is important insofar as we wish to demonstrate that harm is not natural, but results from the conditions and arrangements, actions and practices discussed above. Otherwise the social harm approach finds itself providing some very important descriptive analyses of harm without the necessary conceptual power to explain the origins of harm and the way we may minimise these harms.

Democratic approaches

As the least developed approach, and perhaps more of a strategy for defining social harm rather than constituting a definition per se, democratic approaches draw on experiential knowledge to develop the concept. Hitherto, the definitions discussed emanate from academic debate – they are reliant on expert rather than experiential knowledge. Wilkins (1982), in seeking to develop measures of criminal harms that escape the operation of the criminal law, draws on the notion of social harm. In doing so, he argues that '... the only way to define social harms or grievances is in the terms that the public itself will use' (Wilkins, 1982, p 30). Following the 'basket of commodities' approaches that were previously pioneered in relation to consumer price indexes or standards of living surveys, Wilkins (1982, p 30) suggests that it is possible to generate, through empirical enquiry, a 'meaningful shopping list of events' consisting of 'areas of concern' (personal liberty, individual suffering, human dignity, fear of victimisation) as well as a 'matching list of areas of impact'. He continues to suggest that by identifying a degree of consensus among the public, 'events that are both of frequent occurrence and regarded as serious harms' may then be used to inform the selection of existing statistical measures (Wilkins, 1982, p 31).

Leaving the details of this approach to one side, Wilkins' work serves as a reminder that the definitions that are developed under the banner of a 'social harm' approach must be able to be operationalised in a meaningful sense – those who experience harms or who are witness to these events have important knowledge that must be drawn on to refine 'expert' definitions. In particular, this may be the case when deciding which events cause serious injury, to develop and determine thresholds that indicate whether such an event is harmful or not. Thus, what may emerge from such an approach are hierarchies of harm that prioritise harms that are more injurious than others. Similarly, by drawing on experiential knowledge we understand interrelationships between harms – insofar as social harms have cumulative and additive aspects. However, democratic approaches come with a cautionary caveat attached, in terms of their ability to broaden the sociological lens of harm that the social harm approach is attempting to develop. Given the ideological baggage identified earlier in this book that shapes our perception of harm, solely drawing on 'experiential knowledge' to develop definitions of social harm may result in rather narrow conceptual frames. As alluded to above, it may be that expert definitions are used to frame public dialogue and to open out the possibility for experiential knowledge to validate and further improve these definitions. This would bring us closer to an approach suggested by Kramer, that 'social harms can be best be determined by using some combination of basic human rights as standards, and democratic surveys of what people regard as important social harms' (1985, p 483). This book focuses on developing an 'expert'-derived definition of harm, but future approaches should consider ways that 'expert' definitions could be refined through experiential knowledge.

'Socially mediated' harm

Drawing on the discussion of existing approaches to social harm, this section proposes a definition that will guide the analyses provided within this book. This definition is by no means to be viewed as the 'end position', as Hillyard and Tombs (2004) suggest – such work is ongoing. In other words, it is very much a 'work in progress'. Nevertheless, while the social harm literature may be fragmented, the review of existing works demonstrates discernible themes that emerge from these definitions, to suggest that the formulation of an organising concept for a distinct field of study is entirely possible. It is hoped that the work conducted here will contribute to that process. The book proceeds on the basis that social harm acts *as shorthand to reflect the relations, processes, flows, practices, discourse, actions and inactions that constitute the fabric of our societies which serve to compromise the fulfilment of human needs and in doing so result in identifiable harms*. Framing social harm in this way has three advantages. First, it is not restricted to a single mode of organisation and allows analyses that compare differing varieties of social formation – although, the focus in this book falls on primarily capitalist harm. Second, the definition seeks to capture both the material and relational aspects of harm. And third, the definition allows for structural features of societies through to micro-level human actions to be considered. So an aetiology of social harms may be developed that is able to contextualise micro-level harms, as well as to compare and contrast different sources of harm. However, by setting such broad parameters for the social harm definition without clearly demarcated conceptual boundaries it could become a container for a host of activities that are grievances or irritants, but not necessary injurious. To develop such boundaries requires rules that establish the nature of the social phenomena to be included within the concept.

A starting point for this discussion is to consider how harms may be classified as 'socially mediated'. Through the review of existing literature, an implicit feature of this work suggests that 'socially mediated' harms are considered to encompass avoidable events. In other words, social harms are *preventable* insofar as they remain within human control, or, as Yar (2012) suggests, they fall within the scope of human intervention. The emphasis placed on *preventable* harm is in stark contrast to the more restrictive notion of 'intentional' harm that dominates capitalist ideologies. The prioritisation of 'intentional' harm within the social sciences serves to distort the analysis of harm in two principal ways. First, the notion of intentional harm focuses our attention predominantly on interpersonal harms, therefore rendering invisible harms perpetuated by organisations and social structures. Thus, our 'common-sense' understanding of the harms that pose the greatest threat to our lives and the 'folk devils' who pose these threats is significantly distorted. Second, over the last 30 years the social sciences have come to be dominated by approaches that emphasise the personal biographies of harm at the expense of more structural accounts. By explaining structural harms through discourses of 'risk navigation' or 'resilience', harm is viewed not as the product of alterable social conditions; instead, the victims of harm come to be seen as 'architects of their own demise'. There is a great deal of ideological baggage stacked against structural analyses of harm, largely due to the implications of such an argument for the dominant interests of any given society that benefit from its organisation. Moreover, to consider structures that emerge from the concretisation of historic practices, relations and processes that encompass a seemingly infinite number of actors and decisions appears to defy what is humanly possible. It is against this ideological tide that a notion of *preventable* harm must be developed to provide a rationale for the inclusion of a host of harms that too often fall outside the parameters of social inquiry. A notion of *preventable* harm is articulated as being constituted by either *foreseeable* events or resulting from contexts that are *alterable social relationships*. Let us consider each of these in turn.

Harm can be argued to be preventable if it was foreseeable and therefore could have been avoided. As Presser (2013, p 7) argues:

> Analysts of harm may reasonably study harms that are unintended and unforeseen, as long as the possibility of causing harm was foreseeable. The actors may not have intended to harm but they must have had some notion that their (in) action might result in harm.

This is an important argument to develop to challenge the prioritisation of harms resulting from intentional acts over those that result from social structures. In Friedrich Hayek's (1944/76) discussion of intentionality, we can identify a logic that permeates and structures dominant discourses of harm in capitalist societies. For Hayek, market outcomes could not be considered unjust because the harms that result from them are unintended. Furthermore, Hayek argued that as no consensus could ever be reached over the reallocation of social resources to ameliorate harmful market consequences, there remains no just basis for a state to interfere in such outcomes. An important critique of these ideas can be found in the work of political theorist Raymond Plant (1998, p 67), which allows us to assert that structural harms should be considered to be preventable, exactly because they are foreseeable:

> This argument is defective because our moral responsibility for the consequences of our actions arises not just in relation to the intended consequences but also to the foreseeable consequences.... If the general principle here is

accepted, namely that we are responsible for the foreseeable albeit unintended consequences of our actions, then the issue becomes an empirical one: the extent to which consequences are foreseeable....

Plant's (1988) 'foreseeable consequences' is an important philosophical mechanism to determine whether harm is preventable. However, as Plant suggests, it is the function of empirical analysis to establish whether such harmful consequences were indeed identifiable. Such analysis might point to 'what is already known' about the harmful consequences of particular policies or courses of action, and the availability of alternative, less harmful, strategies that might have been taken.

Even if harms are not *foreseeable*, once knowledge of harm is established, the possibility of human intervention is predicated on the ability to modify the conditions that serve to produce systemic harms. Indeed, the impossibility of such social transformation is often identified as the obstacle to preventing harm, particularly structural harm. We can draw a great deal from Gramsci's understanding of social structure and agency (1971), to advocate a position whereby structural harms are viewed as resulting from *alterable* social arrangements and, therefore, are ultimately preventable instances. This is predicated on our views of structure and agency within society. If we follow Gill's view that social structure is 'a conceptual abstraction that corresponds to how the collective agency of human beings produces regularities that are more or less institutionalised over time and space' (2003, pp 15-16), we may reach a conclusion that 'human beings make society and thus the social world is a human creation.' Thus, we return to a position that lies at the heart of Gramsci's critique of the classic political economists, such as Ricardo, that capitalist markets are neither 'natural' nor 'eternal', but are constituted through the historic mass of habitual collective social actions (1971, p 411). These relations 'are not fixed and immutable, but exist within the dialectics of a given structure ... although social action is constrained by, and constituted within, prevailing social structures, those structures are transformed by agency' (Gill, 2003, p 17). Therefore, notions of social harm must explore the 'limits of the possible' within the parameters of structural constraint to understand the extent to which social arrangements are malleable, and accordingly, harms may come to be viewed as preventable (Gill, 2003, p 17).

How do we discern between harms and non-harms?

It is important that social harm analyses are clear about the distinction between harm as a state, and the harmful situations and processes that give rise to it. There is therefore a potential that social harm becomes tautological, whereby the determining contexts of harm are conflated with specific harm events, and the processes themselves are viewed as harm. Process and outcome must remain analytically distinct. Similarly, for the notion of social harm to gain conceptual rigour, it is critical that criteria are developed that enable a boundary to be drawn between harms and those events that cause annoyance, inconvenience or irritation, but that ultimately are not injurious. Thus we return to Lasslett's claim that his ontological approach 'limits our analysis to the most serious forms of social practice' (2010, p 13). In other words, integral to the notion of social harm is an attempt to capture actions, practices or processes that have a significant impact on our life chances. Naturally, how this is achieved will, of course, be the subject of considerable conjecture, something that is beyond the capabilities of a single study or contribution, but will result from future collective engagements.

The human needs approach to identifying harms arguably offers numerous insights into this ontological question. Any discussion of human need entails an exploration of the facets of being and the material resources, skills, knowledge and social networks that are required for us to be able, as humans, to realise our innate potential. Quite simply, when these needs are not fulfilled, these deficits represent a series of identifiable harms. While it is important that needs are not simply transposed into a concept of social harm, theories of need provide a starting point to begin to develop the rationales and conceptual substance required to demarcate the boundaries of social harm.

Putting to one side the endless list of needs generated by theorists on this topic, for our purposes the most useful aspects of this work are the philosophical discussions that underpin the selection of needs. Notably at the heart of Doyal and Gough's comprehensive exposition of human need is a notion of harm (1991). According to them, harm can be defined either as 'the fundamental disablement in the pursuit of one's vision of the good', or as 'an impediment to successful social participation' (1991, p 50). These are not necessarily mutually exclusive; however, they do represent sufficiently distinct facets of being. On the one hand, 'self-actualisation' is viewed in very instrumental terms, insofar as we are able to design and realise a set of achievable life goals. Then, harms result when we are frustrated in various ways from achieving these goals. On the other hand, harm can be viewed as impediments to 'successful social participation'. Here, social relationships are not merely viewed as a means to an end in the pursuit of our life goals, but are actually an end state with clear intrinsic merit, as a fundamental feature of human existence is 'being with others'.

If we are to avoid harm, to achieve adequate forms of self-actualisation and social participation, specific human needs must be fulfilled. Following this line of argument, the non-fulfilment of specified needs is viewed as constituting either 'disablement' or 'impediments' to successful human action that are manifest in identifiable harms. Therefore, we begin to outline key considerations for the identification of social harms, through the framework offered by the non-fulfilment of needs that must be demonstrated to result in 'disablement' or 'impediment' to successful action or participation. It is from this ontological position that categories of social harm may be built. Here, three main categories of harm are proposed that capture fundamental aspects of this framework: physical/mental health; autonomy; and relational. Each is outlined in turn below.

Physical/mental health harms

As a starting point, it is not controversial to suggest that physical harm resulting in death is a significant 'disablement/impediment' to successful human action or participation; however, this is an unnecessarily restrictive definition of harm. Therefore, the approach adopted here seeks to outline a notion of physical health to guide the identification of physical harm. Thus, physical harm is understood in relation to physical health, in terms of ability to maintain sufficient health so that people may 'lead an active and successful life' (Doyal and Gough, 1991, p 59). This clearly extends beyond mere physical survival, and should be judged through the quality of life available, as life-limiting illness and injury can seriously compromise an individual's ability to exercise their life choices, as well as have an impact on their ability to maintain social relationships. This means that a host of needs must be fulfilled, ranging from access to a healthy diet, access to and time to participate in physical exercise, access to appropriate healthcare systems, adequate shelter and a non-hazardous physical environment to ensure a sufficient level of physical health is maintained. By considering these related needs, they act as resources for people to broaden their comprehension of physical harm, so that they may consider a wide range of physical injuries, disease and conditions as harms.

In terms of mental health harms, there are a range of illnesses and conditions that may be encompassed under this heading. Thus, ranging from extreme psychotic disorders where there may be a complete loss of self and a total inability to participate in social relations, through to clinical forms of depression that manifest in a sense of anxiety over the unpredictably of life, feelings of helplessness and worthlessness. The point is that these conditions result in individuals losing a sufficient degree of control over their lives, and therefore exhibit minimal levels of autonomy. A necessary consideration must be the extent to which societies determine these harms, and the extent to which this may be explained by individual genetic factors.

Autonomy harms

Autonomy harms result from situations where people experience 'fundamental disablement' in relation to their attempts to achieve self-actualisation. Thus self-actualisation is predicated on the achievement of a sufficient level of autonomy insofar as an individual possesses the ability to formulate choices and has the capacity to act on these. There are many harmful ways in which a person's capacity for autonomous action is undermined and self-actualisation frustrated. First, for a capacity for *understanding and learning*, in order to be able to formulate choices and to act on them in an effective manner, people must develop key cognitive skills, such as communication, critical evaluation, as well as a range of intellectual and practical skills. Thus, without effective education systems and opportunities for personal development, an ability to lead lives of one's own choosing remains seriously circumscribed. It is therefore not difficult to demonstrate that illiteracy, innumeracy, and so on, are harms.

Second, self-actualisation is also determined by the *opportunities* people have to engage in meaningful and productive social activity. Self-actualisation and flourishing can be realised through engagement in productive social activities, such as childrearing, and forms of paid work. Thus, a person's sense of self-worth and self-esteem is often derived from their participation and contribution to the division of labour of the society to which they belong. It follows, then, that harm can result from role deprivation, the absence of available opportunities to engage in productive activities. Harms will also result from the performance of roles that remain largely unrecognised and unrewarded, despite the contribution they make to a given society. Similarly, harm can result from role stress, whereby the 'unmanageable conflict between different social roles' prevents effective participation in either (Doyal and Gough, 1991, p 186).

Finally, the ability to *control* the circumstances that have a direct impact on people's lives is fundamental to autonomy and successful human action. This may entail several aspects of human life. A person's civil and political efficacy will largely be dictated by whether they are able to participate in the decisions that affect their life; accordingly, autonomy harms result from situations where people remain powerless in significant decision-making processes. Similarly, an ability to lead relatively autonomous lives will be dependent on the control people exert over sufficient economic and social resources necessary to act on their life choices. When the constancy of these resources are jeopardised, this can feed into harmful states of insecurity that serve to undermine a person's ability to act with confidence or certainty, and to pursue, unhindered, their life choices.

Relational harms

Relational harms come in essentially two forms: harms resulting from enforced exclusion from social relationships, and harms of misrecognition. Dealing with the former first, enforced exclusion from personal relationships and social networks are injurious in many ways. Exclusion from social networks are likely to have an impact on how people are able to function on a day-to-day basis and to perform vital roles, thus, without others to assist with childcare, domestic labour and a range of daily tasks, the likelihood for successful action is limited. Moreover, a person's ability to access opportunities and to develop skills is largely predicated on contact with others. Therefore self-actualisation is not necessarily a product of one's own efforts, but a reflection of how this process is nurtured through supportive networks. Perhaps more fundamentally, few can function for sustained periods of time without maintaining meaningful human relationships and social contacts. These relationships transcend the functionality of everyday life and the contacts made through the division of labour or the exchange of goods and services. Thus, if people are unable to fulfil their emotional needs, such as love and emotional security, it is likely that harms such as loneliness and social isolation will result, as well as associated mental health harms, such as depression. Ultimately, 'being with others' is an essential facet of the human condition – people may choose different forms of association with others, yet without some form of meaningful contact, they are likely to experience a range of harms.

Harms of misrecognition result from the symbolic injuries that serve to misrepresent the identities of individuals belonging to specific social groups. An ability to present one's own identity in the way that they choose is a critical facet of self-actualisation. If 'public identities' are imposed on people by others within society, and presented as 'spoiled' or 'blemished' in one way or another, so that they are viewed as 'other' and therefore distinct from mainstream society, this can have serious consequences for people's ability to participate in society. Moreover, if lifestyles are not viewed as valid within the society in which people live, their ability to follow and exercise choices remains seriously curtailed. In addition, the internalisation of pejorative and stigmatising identities can result in feelings of shame, guilt and humiliation – which are damaging to people's ability to maintain relationships as they may seek to conceal stigmatising aspects of their identity from others or withdraw from particular relationships altogether. A further internalised consequence of stigma is the erosion of self-esteem as an individual assimilates the discourses that set them apart from others – diminishing their self-perception of their contribution and value to society – which has a significant impact on their confidence to formulate and action their life goals.

Limitations of the needs-based approach

It is inevitable that by imposing conceptual order on to the mass of social harms that are produced by capitalist society, that the social harm approach categorises harms. While this may be inescapable for some forms of analysis, it is important to acknowledge the potential drawbacks of such an approach. As Tan (2011) suggests, by focusing our attention on harm as an event, we neglect 'the harmed' as a site of analysis. Perhaps most importantly, through the use of categories, we abstract harm from its original context, and in doing so we can distort the reality of social harm. Thus, it becomes more difficult to understand the interrelated nature of harm, the cumulative impacts of harms across the life course (Pantazis, 2004). Moreover, by focusing on harm and not the harmed, we can also lose sight of the agency of those harmed. Indeed, by focusing on the question of agency, different layers of harm are revealed, whether it be the adaptive harms that Tan suggests result when an individual attempts to 'cope with or respond to harms they are experiencing' (2011, p 182), or counter harms that Tifft and Sullivan argue are 'set in motion by structural violence' but are not '... typically aimed at changing the social arrangements that embody inequality...' (2001, p 193). Understanding these harms requires very different methodological techniques than those demanded by the concerns central to this endeavour, and they are noted but not developed further here.

Similarly, by stepping outside of established discursive frames, the concept of social harm provided runs the risk of being critiqued for relativism. Indeed, it was noted earlier that a recurring critique of the social harm approach is that it lacks objectivity (Tappan, 1947; Cohen, 1993). More recently, Lasslett has raised this critique in relation to needs-based approaches to harm. For Lasslett, needs-based approaches to harm 'confuses harm with injustice' (2010, p 12). Explicitly referring to the author's previous use of Doyal and Gough's theories of need, he suggests that these 'norms ... are ideal forms, which are based upon a certain ethical conception of man ... ideal forms attempt to delineate civilised conditions for social development...' (Lasslett, 2010, p 12). Thus, according to Lasslett (2010, p 12):

> A normative framework will enable the identification of unjust social conditions, which will usually feature instances of socially generated harms, nevertheless, there is no necessary connection between harm and injustice, indeed society may feature many injustices that are not actually harmful.

Lasslett raises an important issue, that harm should be viewed as conceptually distinct from injustice. Behind Lasslett's critique is an implicit assumption that fact and value can be separated; however, it is argued here that such a distinction is neither possible, nor desirable.

First, harm is a value-laden notion. Whatever way you cut it, when we define our subject matter we enter philosophical territory that requires us to make some form of value judgement. It is impossible for us to extricate ourselves from such processes. Fundamentally, when we pose the question 'What is harm?', we are required to engage with the 'ethical conception of man' in order to identify desirable states of being that people are unable to enjoy, but should be able to. In other words, we gain an understanding of harm exactly because it represents the converse reality of an imagined desirable state. In advocating such a stance, this does not mean that social harm dissolves into an intractable subjectivist position, but we are guided by the contingencies and caveats demanded by what is only ever 'humanly objective' (Gill, 2003, p 10). But objectivity does not mean that we avoid ethical norms; it demands that we are clear and realistic about the values that have informed the approach that we take, so that our analyses may be evaluated on this basis.

Second, as Geras argues, 'ethical norms are in no way incompatible with materialist analysis' (1985, p 60); rather, it is fundamental 'to the formation of a desire and for a consciousness for socialism'. Callinicos extends this point, when he suggests 'a theoretically consequent Marxist critique of capitalism requires the articulation of ethical principles in terms of which capitalism is condemned as unjust. How else can it succeed as critique?' (2006, p 221). We may ask the same question of zemiology as a field of study. Thus, we attempt to produce as 'humanly objective' analyses of harm as possible, to describe the conditions in which people exist, but for what purpose? Presumably because we believe harmful conditions contravene some version of the way society 'ought' to be. To remain imprisoned by the legacy of scientism would be a huge error, and it neuters the potency of our critique. Indeed, the 'ought' is likely to be constructed from our analyses of the 'is', as our understanding of the dysfunctional nature of the current state of affairs is derived from the emancipatory imagination of how things could be. Thus, the notion of a 'harm-free society' performs a normative function. Indeed, if we were guided by a Gramscian notion of an 'ethical state' and 'good society', we might begin to understand the ways in which societies may be organised differently to minimise harm, an image against which we may measure historical progress. This is not a prescriptive notion of utopia, but as Gill suggests, a 'normative force' to generate the movement of social change towards a less harmful social form, rather than to 'predict outcome' (2003, p 19).

This also speaks to Garside's criticism that the human needs approach adopted here is ill conceived due to its grounding in a 'static conceptualisation' of the human essence, rather than being historically situated. As an aside, Garside appears to gloss over the tensions within Marx's own writings between the ideas of need and human nature – which assume conflicting relativist and universalist positions (Soper, 1981). If we are to make the critical judgements about capitalism that are necessary to bring about transformative changes to the existing order, we require a criteria for evaluation that is able to transcend historical conjunctures, and therefore exists as a template for critique that applies across time and is not historically relative. Thus, as Doyal and Gough argue, 'to link the expression and satisfaction of "true need" and its satisfaction to systemic revolutionary change while at the same time proclaiming the theoretical impossibility of specifying what the change is meant to achieve – is to live for a future empty of substantive content' (1991, p 28). Thus, human needs-based definitions of harm are key to documenting the destruction and injury current arrangements produce, and how these may be remedied in practice.

Conclusion

This chapter sought to outline the 'lens' used to generate the empirical analyses presented later in this book. It is not intended that the definition is in anyway considered to be definitive; rather, it is hoped that it will contribute to the development of the concept, through its empirical application and subsequent refinement. There is an explicit recognition that the proposed lens based on a conception of the human condition must naturally be couched within a series of caveats. As Chomsky reminds us, critical academics should not be discouraged from engaging with such philosophical discussions; rather, they should 'be bold enough to speculate and create social theories on the basis of partial knowledge, while remaining very open to the strong possibility … that at least in some respects we're very far off the mark' (Foucault and Chomsky, 1997, p 133). Thus, the analyses that result from this lens must be open to the limitations of the lens itself, and so the chapters that follow seek to continually review the empirical application of the lens.

As explained, preventable harms can be considered to be harms that are either foreseeable in nature or result from 'alterable' social conditions. The focus of the remainder of the book falls largely on the latter aspect, as 'foreseeable' harms are somewhat rendered redundant in this instance, as the harms explored in later chapters are well documented and are habitually produced by these societies – therefore, de facto 'foreseeable', given their repeated production. A more important question arises, then, as to whether the systemic production of harm is preventable insofar as these harms can be determined as resulting from 'alterable' social conditions. Thus, what must be established in this case are the ways that it is possible to 'design out' these harms from societies – moving the argument from hypothesis to one grounded in empirical 'fact'. In so doing it will be established that there are no 'natural' levels of harm within societies, and that no harm is inevitable; rather, harms are the outcomes of the way we choose to organise our societies. This also speaks to the assertion that social harm has a transformative capacity, insofar as it is able to not only describe the harms our societies produce, but is capable of articulating visions of alternative, less harmful modes of organisation.

THREE

Capitalist formations and the production of harm

This chapter seeks to progress the argument that structural harms are preventable through further articulating and elaborating the idea that these harms result from 'alterable' social relations. This argument is forged from a position that there are no 'natural' rates of harms within society, and that the experience of harms will vary according to the mode of social organisation that takes hold within a given society. Therefore, if it is possible for nation states to 'organise out' or to reduce harms in comparison to other similarly placed societies, one might conclude that harm is not inevitable; rather, it is a product of 'alterable' social relations. As a starting point for this discussion, it is argued that the organising features of capitalism are inherently harmful, so that the harms that different nation states produce will only vary in extent but not in their nature – indeed, the eradication of harms resulting from capitalist exploitation, alienation and commodification are only possible through alternative social forms. In part, the variation of harms identified between nation states may be explained by the 'embedded' liberal forms that developed in many advanced industrialised nations, following the initial and particularly injurious phases of capitalism, and have served to ameliorate the more harmful aspects of capitalism that result from its 'purest' laissez-faire form. Therefore, the variation in the experience and extent of harm between nation states will depend on the 'embedded' liberal forms that have developed and the nature of the form that harm reduction systems take. With the advent of a variety of neoliberal projects, it is argued that the generative contexts of harm that neoliberal policies create, as well as the dismantling of harm reduction systems, serve to promote more harmful social forms. It is proposed that the impact of neoliberalism has not been uniform, with some formations more receptive to the reforming strategies of these projects. The chapter concludes by developing a 'typology' that seeks to categorise nation states according to the harm reduction characteristics they demonstrate – so that these theoretical arguments may be explored further in the empirical analyses presented in later chapters.

Harmful features of capitalism

A key theme of the book explores varieties of capitalist form and contrasts the harms they produce. It is important that divergence is not overstated and in the process the inherently harmful nature of capitalism is omitted from consideration. As explained above, while the extent of harms may vary, the nature of these harms remains the same. Thus, the fundamental characteristics of harms are replicated across diverse capitalist forms. Indeed, Garside's observations that social harm analyses have, to date, focused on the latest capitalist phase, neoliberalism, at the expense of an analysis of the structural features of capitalism that persist across time and space, is particularly relevant here. As Garside (2013, p 251) convincingly argues, neoliberalism 'offers a poor starting point for understanding the underlying dynamic of the production of social harm'; therefore, Marx's critique of capitalism frames this analysis.

Capitalist systems are often viewed as dynamic social forms driving human progress and civilisation, producing the goods and services that we rely on and could not exist without. Yet, as Marx taught us, the production, distribution and flows of capital that ensure the continuity of these social arrangements also cause widespread harms – in many respects, as the remainder of this section suggests, the production of these harms is a necessary feature of the system (Hillyard and Tombs, 2004). As Garside forcefully reminds us, 'throughout its history the operations of capitalism have been associated with the most profound social harms' (2013, p 252). To avoid rehearsing well-known criticisms of capitalism that Marx's work has given rise to, this section details the key tenets of the critique, and relates these to the three constitutive categories of social harm identified in the previous chapter. In doing so, an argument begins to build that these harms are inherent features of this form of social organisation.

Surplus value and exploitation

Marx's critique of capitalism is predicated on the processes by which surplus value is extracted from the labour–capital relation. Surplus value is derived from the exchange of labour power for a subsistence wage, from which the capitalist receives both the productive activity and creative force of the worker. Ultimately, the worker gives a greater value to the production process than initially existed, for which they receive a fraction of the exchange value of the goods and services created. Thus, all value, be it surplus or profit, results from the exploitation of wage labour. The rate of exploitation, the ratio of surplus to necessary labour time, can be increased in a variety of ways, in either absolute terms through 'squeezing' more from workers through changes to the working day and raising expected levels of output, or, in relative terms, through the introduction of technology to reduce production time and costs. The exploitative nature of these relations forms a generative context from which harms are produced in capitalist societies, in particular, the physical and mental health harms that result from extracting greater levels of productivity from workers that manifest in long working hours, stress-induced conditions, physical illnesses that result from repetitive tasks or long periods spent in particular positions.

Far from being a 'natural' state of affairs, Marx drew our attention to the fetishised nature of this social relation. Thus, despite the appearance of workers' 'freedom' to sell their labour to whomever they choose, as well as consumers' apparent ability to dictate the price that they pay for goods and services, his analysis lay bare the coercion and inequality that exists in the spheres of production and distribution. Essentially, workers within this system face a stark choice – to sell their labour power or to be condemned to the harsh reality of life as part of the reserve army of labour. In doing so, the myth of freedom on which capitalist societies are built is deconstructed, and in so doing, we begin to understand the ways that, for many within these societies, their personal autonomy is compromised in harmful ways. Indeed, the realisation of autonomy under capitalism would appear to be paradoxical in conditions whereby the continued drive for accumulation gives rise to increasing concentrations of social power within the hands of the few. In societies characterised by such stark differentials of power and resources, it is not difficult to envisage the harmful ways in which our autonomy is compromised through the frustration of self-realisation that results in this context. Freedom therefore remains an illusion without the resources and opportunities to realise life goals and plans.

The mode of production – the configuration of the wage labour/capital relation – takes multiple forms and gives rise to the differentiations between workers and the complex hierarchies on which capitalist societies are based. Variance in the mode of production is largely dictated by the value assumed to be contributed by a specific labour form and the means by which surplus value is extracted. For the purposes of the analysis presented, the forms that the modes of production take also vary between different nation states or social formations, insofar as the impediments to the extraction of surplus value – such as the collective organisation of workers – diverge in important and significant ways. Therefore, our experience of harms – the physical impacts and the ways in which our autonomy is compromised – will vary in intensity according to different modes of production, as some will be more humane than others; however, they remain injurious all the same.

Alienation

For Marx, the injurious consequence of the extraction of surplus value and exploitation is the alienation workers endure within the sphere of production. A fundamental characteristic of being human is our ability to consciously engage in work as an activity that is rewarding and productive, that has the potential to contribute to our self-development. Thus, work in the capitalist system 'is external to the worker, that it is not a part of his nature, that consequently he does not fulfil himself in his work but denies himself, has a feeling of misery, not of well being, does not develop freely a physical and mental energy, but is physically exhausted and mentally debased' (Marx, 1844/1963, p 177). However, in the words of Marx, 'the alienated character of work ... appears in the fact that it is not his work but work for someone else, that in work he does, does not belong to himself but to another person' (p 178). Within this system the worker loses control over what is produced from their labour, as well as the process of production itself. This process of alienation perpetuates autonomy harms, as our ability for self-actualisation is compromised when we do not have opportunities to engage in meaningful and productive work of our own choosing.

Alienation extends far beyond the sphere of production to provide a broader context that generates further harms. As Ferguson et al (2002, p 76) note, 'whilst there is a group in society that wields an enormous amount of power ... the vast experience of working class people is an experience not of power but rather of powerlessness, of having little or no control over major areas of their lives.' Thus, a host of autonomy harms result when we lose control of the decisions that affect our lives and the resources necessary to act on our life choices. Furthermore, the alienating nature of the system creates divides between those who gain and those who are exploited, alongside the competition it encourages that pits individuals against one another to improve their 'lot', which clearly militates against feelings of solidarity towards others, and undermines the possibilities for collective interests to form. Individualism within capitalist societies erodes an essential aspect of the human condition – 'being with others' – and so the high degrees of individualisation and fragile social cohesion that pervades these societies also results in a host of relational harms. These can result from the difficulties experienced in making and sustaining meaningful relationships with friends and family that manifest in forms of social isolation and loneliness.

Commodification

Capitalism strips us bare, reducing our worth as human beings to the sum of the contribution we are perceived to make to the processes of accumulation. In its most unrefined form, where human needs are almost entirely subjugated to the needs of capital, dehumanisation can be unremitting and is undoubtedly injurious. 'Commodity fetishisation' obscures the consequences of the prioritisation of capital over human needs. Thus, it renders invisible social relationships between capital and workers, so that these relationships appear to be between 'objects' or 'entities', therefore reducing workers to the status of a mere 'component' or 'unit' among others, such as machinery or land, that constitute the production process. This provides a generative context through which workplace harms are produced, if workers are to be viewed as a 'unit' in the production process, as with any 'unit' they are subject to 'calculus' that seeks to extract the greatest levels of productivity and profit from each aspect of the process. Such 'calculus' or 'cost benefit analyses' are amoral in nature, rendering actors indifferent to the injurious implications of 'business decisions' that prioritise profit above human needs. There are numerous case studies of the physical harms that result from 'business decisions' that have utilised the amoral calculus of 'cost benefit analyses' that foreground profit over safety concerns for workers and consumers.

However, commodification is not only a feature of the sphere of production in capitalist society; it extends well beyond this sphere to have an impact on many areas of our lives. As Slapper and Tombs (1999, p 144) note:

> Capitalism relentlessly reduces all forms of social relationships into economic ones; in this sense, the development of capitalism is synonymous with the commodification of all forms of human life.

The extension of this logic into broader societal spheres has harmful consequences. First, commodification serves to undermine social solidarity, the social bonds and ties that exist despite the individualist impulses of capitalist relations to humanise these societies. Harm production in capitalist societies will be influenced by the extent to which forms of social solidarity are able to decommodify aspects of social life. As argued later in the chapter, societies that are more solidaristic in nature are likely to demonstrate greater empathy for others and, in turn, develop social security systems, regulatory agencies and so on, that serve to protect against the more rapacious and harmful aspects of commodification in capitalist societies. Second, commodification provides a generative context for many relational harms. Our worth as members of society is often evaluated through our perceived 'economic' contribution. Therefore, the 'victim status' attributed to those who experience harm will be determined as a result of their perceived 'worth'. The existence of autonomy harms, such as poverty, tends to be legitimated through discourses that construct those who endure these harms as 'architects of their own demise', as worth and identity is almost solely determined in capitalist societies by the paid work that is performed. Therefore the societal stigma and pejorative discourses that come to be attached to 'worklessness', 'the receipt of state benefits' or 'low income' can manifest in feelings of shame, guilt and humiliation that undermine self-esteem, thus compromising ability to flourish.

Crises of capital/ism

Capitalism's much celebrated dynamism results from the profit motive that compels individuals to compete against one another for similar ends – a motivational structure that imbues the system with a degree of coherence. However, it is the uncoordinated nature of competitive accumulation that gives rise to a host of contradictions within capital, which more often than not result in crisis. The history of capitalism is littered with periodic crises and bears witness to its inherently volatile and unstable form. According to Marx, crisis is an inevitable and unavoidable consequence of capitalism's chaotic and anarchic form, with each crisis proving necessary for the system to purge itself of obstacles and blockages. Marx portrays a system that generates contradictions that primarily result from the oscillations of under/overproduction, that are then absorbed into other areas of the system, such as the financial system, in order to reverse falling levels of profit. Yet the readjustments such crises generate remain temporary patches, insofar as different terrains within the capitalist system absorb these contradictions, but then these contradictions only subsequently play out in a new terrain, and, as Harvey remarks, 'can spin onwards and outwards in this way to encompass every aspect of the capitalist mode of production' (2007b, p 32). Ultimately, capitalist crises perform an important function, resetting the conditions for accumulation in either specific circuits of capital or more widely, depending on the nature of the crisis.

But while crises may be necessary to bring 'equilibrium' to the system, they are also responsible for an array of harms. As Gamble (2009, p 47) notes, 'one of the key functions of the crisis for Marx was to reconstitute what he called the reserve army of labour, by making thousands of workers unemployed … and driving down wages'. While resetting the labour relation serves to restore the conditions necessary for accumulation, it also provides generative contexts for the production of autonomy harms. Crises 're-impose' discipline on labour, serving as a persuasive discursive tool to 'free' labour markets of regulatory impediment that protect working conditions, pay and hours. More broadly, in response to specific crises, capital has sought to reconfigure its relationship with the state; this may be through processes of deregulation of markets or to remove 'burdens' in the forms of corporate taxation from business. Indeed, the state itself has contracted, reducing expenditure on benefits or service provision, often seeking to rebalance the relationship between the public and private sectors of the economy, so the former does not 'crowd out' the latter. At these points we tend to witness the dismantling of the state's 'harm reduction' capacity, which itself generates a host of harms, such as increased poverty, homelessness and so on. Regardless of the function that crises perform, they create conditions that are harmful, precipitating often acute deterioration of living standards, limiting opportunities for economic participation and creating greater levels of anomie. Thus, 'secondary harms' tend to result in times of crisis, with considerable evidence linking recession to increased physical and mental health harms such as suicide, murder and mental illness, that result from increases in unemployment and financial insecurity.

Varieties of capitalism, varieties of harm production?

If we move beyond the underlying nature of capitalist harm, important points of variation exist, insofar as the intensity and extent of these harms vary dramatically according to the type of capitalist formation. Thus, as argued above, different modes of production may result from contrasting forms of political and social organisation, and in turn, these determine a variety of outcomes. Fundamental to developing an understanding of the contrasting organisation of capitalist societies is the role attributed to the state. Indeed, the role of the state is a recurring theme, in particular, the interplay between state and capital. These concepts form the basis of the discussion in this chapter and are further elaborated throughout; it is important, however, to briefly outline the ways in which the state is approached.

The state is viewed as a terrain through which social forces and interests are acted out. As Poulantzas (1978, p 132) argued, the state should be considered to be a 'material condensation' of the forces that constitute the historical bloc. However, he warns us that 'the state is not reducible to the relationship of forces; it exhibits an opacity and resistance of its own', thus guaranteeing the relative autonomy of state apparatus and its unique qualities (1978, p 130). At any point, then, the state is constituted by a delicate balance of forces giving rise to the contingent and unstable nature of state power. Thus, the state is not a monolithic entity: 'internal cracks, divisions and contradictions of the state do not represent mere dysfunctional accidents' but are representative of a field of struggles (Poulantzas, 1978, p 132). If the state is conceived as a field of struggles through which social relations come to be contested, it is possible to conceive of ways in which 'claims for social justice and progressive politics are forged, fought over, resisted and implemented' (Coleman et al, 2009, p 14).

When the state is viewed in this way, it allows an exploration of the contradictory and complex relationship between the state and the production of capitalist harm. Nation states are often *complicit* in capitalist harms through the role they play in the maintenance and reproduction of inequitable social orders. As Poulantzas (1978) notes, the state has a considerable capacity to organise aspects of capitalist society. Without the organising frameworks of 'dispossession' – through which public goods are converted into private property – and 'exploitation' – that regulate the labour–capital relation – provided by the state, the conditions necessary for wealth accumulation would not be possible, and neither would the harmful contexts of capitalist organisation. Principally, the juridical power wielded by states is crucial to these frameworks in a variety of ways: through the regulatory structures that create and sustain markets, where otherwise profit-making would not be possible, such as privatised rail systems, utilities or telecommunications; or the right to private property realised through civil law, that ensure that the contracts that arise from the sale of goods and services are honoured. Underpinning this juridical power is the state's capacity for monopolised physical violence. Indeed, the more coercive expressions of state power are deployed when conflicts arise from the inequitable conditions of capitalist society, be it from the labour–capital relation or through the maldistribution of resources and goods – to ensure the conditions for accumulation and rights to private property are secured. Nation states' use of 'legitimate' physical violence, and their immense capacity to perform violent acts, is an obvious and much documented source of harms.

However, as previously asserted, the state is a contradictory site that does not simply reflect dominant interests, but necessarily provides spaces of contestation, that absorb and respond to progressive politics. Therefore, while the state may be *complicit* in capitalist harm production, it also creates structures that serve to *mediate/ameliorate* harms. Even from the earliest, most avaricious, phase of capitalism in the 19th century, a number of structures emerged that served to address the chaos of laissez-faire capitalism's externalities and the resulting collateral harms. Despite the prevailing liberal rhetoric of the minimalist state, that appeared to guide the emergent forms of public and social policy, the reality of harm caused by unfettered capitalism resulted in the incremental development of aspects of contemporary harm reduction systems. Taking the example of the UK, systems of regulation around pollution (Alkali Acts), health and safety (Factory Acts) begin to evolve, as well as public health, pensions, social security and workers' insurance that emerge from the 19th century and initial years of the 20th century (Fraser, 2009).

Through the incremental evolution of these structures, we witness the hegemonic function of the state in relation to capitalist harm. Thus, left to its own devices, capitalism is both volatile and destructive. In order to prevent the system descending into chaos, an important aspect of the state's hegemonic role in relation to harm is to prevent and provide redress for the collateral harms resulting from capitalist organisation. In order to cement the diverse groups within the historical bloc, a fundamental aspect of the state's hegemonic role is to explain and legitimate the harms arising from the organisation of capitalist society, in order to guarantee the impossibility of the disintegration of this bloc, and to secure the interests of those who benefit from these arrangements. Without these discursive formations, the harmful nature of capitalist organisation comes to be challenged, and alternative, less harmful, forms of existence take hold within the imaginations of those subordinate groups that constitute the bloc.

Globalisation, neoliberalism, convergence and variation

In recent years, much has been written about the role and capacity of the nation state. The purpose of this section is not to rehearse well-trodden debates on these subjects, but to consider the implications of these developments for the ability of nation states to *mediate/ameliorate* harms. More specifically, the state has arguably faced two related challenges in this regard. These result from both the enmeshment of processes that transcend nation states, crystallising into forms of *globalisation* that are said to weaken the standing of nation states, as well as the emergence to hegemonic dominance of the political project of *neoliberalism* that has seemingly coerced nation states into increasingly convergent forms. Each of these developments are looked at in turn, but should be considered to be interrelated.

First, it is assumed by many commentators that the mobility of capital and production in an increasingly interconnected global world serves to undermine the ability of nation states to formulate and implement policies that would control and diminish harm production. Numerous writers have portrayed a 'constrained state' operating within an era of globalisation, to be reduced to the function of ensuring the 'rule of law, basic regulation and minimum safety nets' (Weiss, 2003, p 3). Cerny et al (2005) suggest that globalisation has created a host of pressures for nation states, through the mobility of finance capital, the emergence of tax havens, the development of global chains of production – in turn, these appear to consolidate the power of corporations and wealthy individuals. Thus states are reduced to 'competition states' that seek to make production and the location of profits and assets as attractive as possible to corporations and wealthy individuals, by minimising the burdens placed on wealth accumulation. In theory, these developments should weaken the capacity of states to insulate their populations from harms, and create conditions that are harm-generative, by limiting the funds available for regulatory regimes and social security systems, and to place ideological limits on the regulatory fetters and limits that can be placed on the exploitative nature of capitalism. Thus, trends in the harm protection/reduction features of capitalist states should, according to the logic of these arguments, appear to be converging towards a restricted and minimalist form.

Globalisation has come to be viewed as a series of pressures and constraints, and these are not without contestation. It is undisputable that economic interdependence has increased over the last 30 years, yet the ramifications for nation states must be subject to critical scrutiny. For many, the untrammelled advance of globalisation and its economic forces are overstated and, therefore, the implications of globalisation for nation states dramatised for ideological purposes (Callinicos, 2001). Numerous empirical analyses have sought to examine the 'realities' of globalisation, and point to contrasting facets of the phenomena, either to support or to reject the weakened state thesis. Reviewing this empirical evidence reveals a complex and contradictory picture, whereby the pressure points brought to bear on nation states are unevenly distributed. It is important to fully understand the material reality of these economic forces to understand the 'constraints' placed on nation states, as well as the 'opportunities' for states to dictate policy responses to capitalist harm. Thus, economic enmeshment is not comprehensive or complete, but patchy and varied. As sceptics suggest, 'trade, capital and investment flows ... are still primarily national in scope' (Weiss, 2003, p 13). However, finance capital appears to have had a far greater disciplinary impact on nation states. Again, Weiss (2003) urges caution about generalising these impacts, identifying specific constraints that have been placed on discrete policy areas, in particular, public borrowing to fund social expenditure, and neither are these universally felt, with greater pressure inevitably placed on countries with more 'open' economies.

The complex nature of this material reality is somewhat at odds with the 'common-sense' political orthodoxy that has raised to hegemonic 'truth' the constraints imposed by globalisation on nation states. Thus, the political construction of 'helplessness' of nation states in the face of globalisation has created a new discursive terrain that constrains 'the possible, the desirable and the feasible' for nation states (Hillyard and Tombs, 2004, p 40). While these discourses have been incredibly persuasive, shaping the policy agendas of many nation states, there are important spaces of contestation within the current hegemony of advanced capitalist societies that are worthy of examination.

First, the construction of helplessness creates a perverse irony, that populations become more aware of the risks attached to globalisation, and the volatility associated with finance capital and speculation, as well as 'footloose' production, creates heightened feelings of insecurity. This sense of insecurity generated by both the material realities (as well as the mythology) of globalisation generates a set of internal pressures on nation states and political elites from different sections of its electorate for protection from the harms generated by the new global economic order.

Second, nation states are of fundamental importance to the organisation of regional and global markets; without regulatory structures, or legal systems of contract or patents, current forms of wealth accumulation would not be possible. Thus, it is more appropriate to consider a symbiotic relationship between transnational capital and advanced industrial states, whereby states guarantee the conditions necessary for accumulation, a point underlined by the global credit crunch, where in the immediate aftermath, many nation states acted to 'bail out' failing financial institutions and to ensure that the flow of capital within domestic economies did not entirely seize up. As the repercussions of reduced liquidity came to be experienced in other sectors of national economies, nation states were equally required to shore up sectors of the manufacturing industry, through a host of government-financed schemes, to guarantee demand – particularly in the initial phase of the credit crunch, the car manufacturing industry was supported in the UK through a 'scrappage guarantee' scheme. Similarly, stuttering housing markets in the US and UK have been underwritten through government-funded mortgage guarantee schemes. In recent years, the nation state has demonstrated its considerable capacity to act, to ensure the continuation of capitalism as we know it, which gives some purchase to analyses that assert the relative autonomy of nation states to create policy – in particular, harm reduction policies.

The increased interdependency of national economies that has characterised the era of globalisation was arguably facilitated by the economic liberalisation that removed trade barrier tariffs and monetary controls surrounding national economies, and occurred from the 1970s onwards in the name of neoliberalism. Yet, the growth of supranational organisations synonymous with the contemporary phase of globalisation, such as the International Monetary Fund (IMF), World Trade Organization (WTO) and The World Bank, have been at the forefront of promulgating neoliberal ideas as a mode of governance. A key question to be addressed in this book is the extent to which varieties of capitalism continue to exist, and more specifically, distinct models of harm reduction, or whether they have converged around more harmful versions of neoliberal capitalism than existed under 'embedded liberal' forms. The discussion that follows seeks to clarify how neoliberalism will be addressed in the book, and in particular, the relationship between harm production and neoliberalism.

Neoliberalism is an often-used term; however, it is ambiguously and loosely deployed in many instances, and it is necessary to clarify its use here. Neoliberalism, as Harvey (2007a, p 19) correctly puts it, should be viewed as a 'political project to re-establish the conditions for capital accumulation and to restore the power of economic elites', and, therefore, to reverse the gains made by the working classes in many advanced nations after the Second World War. In doing so, Harvey (2007a) is at pains to distinguish between the 'utopian project' that emanates from neoliberal ideologues to assert the primacy of the market as a vehicle for social progress, and the political project that sought to restore power to the elites. For Harvey, the former serves to legitimate the latter, which is demonstrated by the fact that when these distinct projects conflict, the ideals are readily dispensed with – as was evidenced in the early phase of the credit crunch when 'market fundamentalists', particularly in the US, castigated Obama's bail out of the financial sector for not following the 'orthodoxy', arguing that following the short, sharp, shock of the crash, markets would quickly achieve equilibrium having purged themselves of the weaker financial institutions.

Returning to Harvey's historical point (2007a), neoliberalism emerged as a political project in the midst of the crises of the 1970s, and signalled the retreat of embedded liberalism in various nation states, as well as the abandonment of Keynesian economics. As Peck et al (2010, p 108) suggest, neoliberalism was 'conceived and born as a crisis theory' to seize the opportunity when the rupture in the Keynesian hegemony occurred, and has since evolved into a host of separate and distinct state projects that have developed through their relationship to crises, insofar as the crises of the 1970s 'precipitated deregulation which culminated, in later crises' that led to calls for re-regulation, signalling the growth of multiple forms of neoliberalism. As Önis and Güven (2011, p 472) note, following the East Asian financial crisis, international financial institutions, such as the IMF and World Bank, began advocating a more 'social, regulatory and pragmatic neoliberalism' – arguably a model of neoliberalism that gained greater purchase in the immediate aftermath of the credit crunch. Thus there are many adaptations and deviations from the orthodox, laissez–faire position, largely due to the unpalatable and implausibility of the application of this doctrine; therefore it is important not to think of neoliberalism as one form, but as a series of multiple localised versions.

Peck et al's observation that neoliberalism is best viewed as a 'hegemonic restructuring ethos ... a dominant pattern of regulatory transformation, and not as a fully coherent system' (2010, p 104) helps us reach an understanding of the ways in which neoliberalism has produced numerous localised variants. Moreover, by viewing neoliberalism 'in an essentially parasitical relationship with ... extant social formations with which it has an antagonistic relationship', we are reminded by Peck et al (2010, p 104) to consider the contingencies that arise from this hegemonic relation. Thus, the 'restructuring ethos' of neoliberalism may be contested and resisted to varying degrees through the unique institutional architecture and political traditions of different nation states. However, where 'host' social formations appear to be more closely aligned to the principles of neoliberalism, 'restructuring', arguably, has had its greatest impact. The idea that neoliberalism has prompted states to converge towards a minimal state form must be treated with caution, as it follows that some social formations demonstrate considerable resilience towards the logic of neoliberal restructuring. Thus, within this context, the empirical investigations of this book seek to explore points of convergence and variance between different nation states' harm reduction structures, and the extent to which these structures have been reconfigured or dismantled according to neoliberal logic. We return to this discussion in greater detail later in the chapter.

Peck et al (2010) allow us to conceive of neoliberalism as a 'restructuring' force that has gained material purchase in numerous iterations, yet it remains for the purposes of clarity that a definition of neoliberalism is offered here to guide readers through the remainder of the text. Hay's (2004) seven-point definition of neoliberalism attempts to capture the 'core precepts', but is 'sufficiently general' to capture the variants that Peck et al (2010) highlight, and for this reason it is deployed here. To paraphrase, Hay suggests that neoliberalism can be identified according to the following traits:

> (1) A confidence in the market as an efficient mechanism for the allocation of scarce resources.... (2) A belief in the ... global regime of free trade and free capital mobility.... (3) A belief in ... a limited and non interventionist role for the state and of the state as a facilitator and custodian rather than a substitute for market mechanisms.... (4) A rejection of Keynesian demand management techniques in favour of monetarism, neo monetarism and supply side economics.... (5) A commitment to the removal of those welfare benefits which might be seen to act as disincentives to market participation.... (6) A defence of labour–market flexibility and the promotion and nurturing of cost-competitiveness.... (7) A confidence in the use of private finance in public projects and more generally, in the allocative efficiency of market and quasi market mechanisms in the provision of public goods. (Hay, 2004, pp 507-8)

It is hypothesised here that neoliberalism is a particularly harmful version of capitalism, that it has sought to dismantle the harm reduction systems that flourished as a result of 'embedded liberalism'. In many respects, neoliberalism erodes the more humane capitalist forms that developed in advanced industrialised nations, to reveal the inherently harmful characteristics of capitalism that hitherto were ameliorated through 'embedded liberal' forms. The purpose of the following subsections is to sketch the assumed harmful facets of the neoliberal project.

Competition

Competition imbues capitalism with its inherently volatile nature, making it 'crisis' prone. Thus, as capitalism has evolved, various attempts have been made to temper this volatility. 'Embedded liberalism' arises in various forms, from the beginning of the 20th century in many advanced capitalist societies, and gathers momentum after the Second World War to mediate the excesses of market economies, by establishing mechanisms and strategies that resulted in more collaborative and coordinated capitalist forms. Neoliberalism sought to replace the 'socialisation of economic activity' undertaken by 'embedded liberalism' with a distinctly individualised form, which O'Connor (2010, p 691) has termed 'coercive competition'. Coercive competition has taken hold through the manipulation of 'insecurities' in relation to 'footloose capital' and 'global chains of production', introducing new global competitors into domestic markets, that hitherto, according to the globalisation discourse, did not exist. Thus, coercive competition provides the 'mechanism whereby union concessions, welfare retrenchment, corporate reorganisation, labour market flexibility ... are extracted', and in doing so offers a series of discursive logics that undermine structures, prima facie designed to control the production of harm or to mediate the consequences of capitalist harms (O'Connor, 2010, p 698).

But perhaps just as importantly, 'coercive competition' has far wider-ranging implications, insofar as it provides the generative context of harm production in many contemporary capitalist societies. The logic of 'coercive competition' is not confined to economic activity, but extends to all areas of social life, and therefore serves to undermine existing forms of social solidarity, which provide the collective will through which many harm reduction structures come to be organised. As social solidarity erodes, our bonds weaken, and concern for the other dissipates, thus our indifference to the suffering of others increases – interventions in the systemic harms produced by capitalist harm become less organised and increasingly sporadic. Moreover, highly atomised societies that pitch individuals against one another in a zero sum game generate anomie at all levels of society – not just among the 'precariat', who are increasingly denied legitimate opportunities to achieve the formal goals of capitalist society, but also corporate actors who operate within regulatory vacuums pursuing profit, with little thought for the consequences of their actions.

Structural power of capital

The neoliberal project, as characterised by Harvey (2007a), has sought to reverse gains and concessions secured through 'embedded liberalism' after the Second World War in many advanced nation states. Dumenil and Levy's analysis of assets and income in the US (2004) demonstrate the huge shifts in wealth to the top 1 per cent of US society that has been undertaken since the 1970s. Neoliberalism in many countries has reconfigured the very structures of our societies, through changes to taxation systems, driving down the value of benefits and wages, and diminishing the availability and quality of public services. This redistribution of economic wealth has been accompanied by the rebalancing of political power, which has been achieved through the undermining of trade unionism in many countries. In the UK, from 1979, nine Acts of Parliament in 13 years dramatically curtailed union activity and those workers covered by collective bargaining agreements (Hutton, 1995). These factors have coalesced to enhance the structural power of capital, reconfiguring the balance of forces in many late capitalist societies, thus creating a hegemonic terrain where greater pressure is exacted on the harm reduction systems embedded within capitalist societies – providing contexts where the fetters these systems place on accumulation have been contested, and in many cases, dismantled.

Under the ideological auspices of neoliberalism, many nation states have sought to privatise publicly owned utilities and services. Free market dogma dictated this would not only improve the efficiency of the service in question, but would also open out new avenues of commercial activity that had hitherto been 'crowded out' as a result of state ownership. Thus, the 1980s and 1990s saw the sale of many of these utilities into private ownership. Harvey (2007b) has likened this process to 'primitive accumulation', whereby these utilities and resources were taken from common ownership and placed into the hands of private capital – often sold for less than their market value. In many countries, these markets have become dominated by monopoly providers, the energy markets being a clear example, where competition appears to have resulted in monopoly. Thus, in many nation states, the delivery of essential services is now controlled by markets or a few oligarchs, and in turn, guided by concerns for profit rather than to meet human needs.

But more fundamentally, societies characterised by intense inequalities are particularly harmful. Inequality creates contexts where harms are not just unequally distributed, but lead to the increased experience of physical harms, for example, homicide, obesity and premature deaths, as well as autonomy harms, as highly unequal societies have lower rates of social mobility (Wilkinson and Pickett, 2010). Moreover, the rapacious growth of inequality in capitalist societies arguably only serves to intensify the underlying processes of alienation that are a fundamental feature of capitalism, with worker representation greatly diminished, and tripartite systems of industrial relations eroding – many workers are far removed from the decisions that have an impact on their working lives. As the value of wages and benefits decrease, entire populations are excluded from spheres of social activity, including consumption of goods and services through which our identities are so readily formulated in contemporary capitalist society. Thus, the inequalities generated through neoliberalism have only served to increase for many the sense of powerlessness in capitalist society.

Financialisation

From the late 1970s and 1980s, the US and UK led the deregulation of financial markets, with national systems becoming increasingly integrated into global stock and financial trading markets. Inevitably, financial centres began to compete to provide the most attractive (or least regulated) places to invest – providing a set of downward pressures among the financial centres to further deregulate – which created immense volatility within these markets. The growth in financialisation was driven by what Harvey (2010, p 29) notes to be a 'peculiar' problem, 'low wages and low profits', insofar as the 'deregulation' of labour markets had exerted downward pressure on the real value of wages, which was, in turn, to be remedied through the financial sector and the credit card industry replacing lost income through cheap credit. Thus, those who had been considered too risky in the past had a panoply of credit cards, store cards, mortgages offered to them, and these risks could be 'disappeared' from the books of financial institutions through increasingly inventive forms of 'securitisation'. In terms of low profits, or more precisely, declining rates of production values, the problem for capital of where to locate surplus came increasingly to be solved via the investment in asset values. As surplus value was converted rapidly into finance capital, a host of inventive and risky practices were sought to dispose of this capital. As Harvey puts it, 'new markets arose, pioneered within what became known as the shadow banking system, permitting investment in credit swaps, currency derivations, and the like ... the futures market embraced everything from trading in pollution to betting on the weather' (2010, p 21).

Depending on the level of integration into these financial systems, nation states and their populations were left vulnerable to these volatile and crisis-prone markets. Indeed, prior to the credit crunch, the volatility of speculative finance capital was patently clear from the East Asian and Dot.Com crises; however, the impacts of these had remained localised, and business continued as normal. For the few, these markets generated even greater wealth than they had before; for bankers and traders charged with the responsibility of making this capital 'work', they were equally well rewarded. However, the failure of these markets and the crises they have precipitated have caused harm on an inconceivable scale, ranging from the loss of pensions and savings through to the recessions that followed from the credit crunch that resulted in unprecedented levels of unemployment and dramatic falls in living standards, to the near bankruptcy of national governments.

Statecraft

Alongside the 'free economy' envisaged by the neoliberal project lies a specific vision of the state, or as Gamble (1988) terms it, 'the strong state'. Thus, the state is conceived as the 'nightwatchman', operating at the margins of the economy to ensure markets operate freely, and to ensure both our physical security as well as private property. The work of Poulantzas in particular (1978) alerts us to the historical emergence of the 'strong state' during the 1970s in many nation states to replace elements of the 'social state' that flourished as a result of 'embedded liberalism'. The argument here is not that the 'social state' withers away entirely at this point; it is more the case that in many societies, the balance between the 'coercive' and 'beneficent' features of the state has been reconfigured in favour of the former (Supiot, 2013).

Thus, in the UK Thatcherism's remoulding of the state insinuated an unstinting faith in the market as a force for social 'good'. Here, the market was to be 'freed' from the meddling of state bureaucrats and the perceived power of the unions, low inflation was to be maintained and wealth accumulation rewarded. These aims were to be achieved through an extensive privatisation programme, the disciplining of the trade unions, taxation cuts for the wealthy, reductions in benefit levels for lone parents and children, and the removal of some benefits for selected groups, such as young people. The impact of welfare retrenchment and changes to taxation were reflected in the demonstrable increases in poverty and inequality during this period (Gordon and Pantazis, 1997). Increasingly, the criminal justice system has been used to deal with social problems and tensions within capitalist society, replacing the longstanding attachment to the welfare state and corporatist politics.

The point is that the reconfiguration of the state in these ways has identifiable impacts on the harm reduction institutions and mechanisms that flourished particularly following 1945 in many nations, as described earlier in this chapter. Thus, 'fetters' on market activity, often referred to as 'red tape', such as regulatory systems that served to enforce labour standards in relation to health and safety or pay, or that regulated industrial pollutants, were subject to reform to readjust the 'burdens' these systems placed on business. Moreover, welfare states and criminal justice systems came to be reconfigured through a renewed emphasis on individual rather than collective responsibility for harms, so that the generosity and coverage of welfare payments and services diminish, while the criminal justice expands as an institution of exclusion rather than rehabilitation. Ultimately, the extent to which states have been subject to neoliberal statecraft will determine the forms that respective harm reduction systems take.

Harm reduction regimes

So far the chapter has presented a series of arguments that suggest capitalism is an inherently harmful form, but different capitalist forms vary in relation to the extent and experience of these harms. This section outlines a typology of nation states that seeks to categorise nations according to identifiable characteristics of harm reduction. It draws on different systems, such as welfare, criminal justice and regulation, as well as broader social relations, such as social solidarity, to classify nation states in relation to these factors, the purpose being to be able to generate theories that are able to explain the variance of harms between advanced capitalist societies, as well as to provide tools that can capture such divergence empirically.

Through constructing different 'stylised' ideal types of harm reduction systems, we begin from an assumption that there are a variety of capitalist modes, while there remain sufficient commonalities between those nation states that are allotted to specific regime types. Whether convergence, in terms of the increased homogeneity of the characteristics of harm reduction systems in capitalist societies, has actually occurred and continues to do so, will only be able to be mapped if a hypothetical, and in turn, empirical, starting point, is established from which trends can then be discerned. But only by reducing societies to their defining characteristics, or, as Arts and Gelisson (2002, p 140) suggest, to impose a 'simplification and aloofness from detail', is it possible to gain an overview, a schematic sense of societies through which comparisons can be formulated that is reliant on identifying the 'totality' of harm reduction systems. Ultimately, while we forego the complexity and depth offered by single country case studies (Crouch and Streeck, 1997) that draw our attention to the often contradictory nature of national systems, as Esping-Anderson (1999, p 73) puts it, such typologies 'helps us see the forest rather than myriad trees'. Thus, if it is possible to cluster nation states according to harm reduction characteristics, then we can begin to identify the underlying patterns that determine the forms and extent of harm produced within different societies. From this position, we can begin to build theories systematically through the generation and subsequent testing of harm hypotheses – which is an important consideration given the emergent nature of knowledge in this area. More specifically, the movement from 'ideal types' to empirical 'impure types' begins to generate understanding. The continual movement between reality and concept is, therefore, a creative and productive process – viewed in this way, the use of ideal types are a 'means to an end' (Arts and Gelissen, 2002, p 140).

Naturally, some nation states within the same 'family types' are likely to conform to different degrees to the characteristics of the ideal types. It is anticipated that some nation states are a better fit than others, and that they are likely to be positioned at different points along a 'continuum'. Again, the 'fit' is important to develop our understanding of the distribution of harm and the factors that influence these levels; it may be that societies diverge on an important singular aspect that can explain contrasting experiences of harm in these societies. Thus, the notion of a continuum within families serves to acknowledge for some nation states that they are a closer 'fit' to the ideal type, and that, ultimately, some nation states are purer forms than others – this is not a problem for the typologies, as long as these differences are identified and understood. Determining the 'fit' between 'ideal' and 'impure' types requires 'stepping back' methodologically to assess the totality of harm reduction systems, and to not allow contradictory isolated policy areas to undermine classification. However, where the totality of the system appears to contradict the ideal type, it may be that a different ideal type is required, or an entirely new type developed.

There are numerous critiques of the use of ideal types to capture varieties of capitalist organisation. First, as Hancke et al (2007) note, the methodological primacy afforded to nation states tends to view them as being 'hermetically sealed' and, as a result, 'neglects the linkages between them and the forces of convergence' (p 7), a conclusion that is supported by Cerny et al (2005), when they argue that such typologies of nation states can 'overstate difference', and in so doing fail to 'capture international homogenisation'. It is certainly a potential pitfall of ideal types, based on an assumption of variety, that an undue emphasis is placed on divergence rather than increasing similarities between nation states; however, it is unclear how we are to arrive at a conclusion of homogeneity – if we do not map the differences as a starting point, it is difficult to see how the direction of travel can be evaluated.

Second, a number of critiques have focused on the 'static' nature of ideal types that appear to presuppose 'stability' that fails to take account of the dynamics of change (Deeg and Jackson, 2007), and therefore overstates path dependence (Hancke et al, 2007). This is an important point, as it raises the question of how best to capture the mutations that occur over time, as well as to understand the shifting forces that prompt such reconfigurations in capitalist formations. This becomes an empirical issue, whereby the 'totality' of the practices and social institutions must be evaluated and contrasted to an 'ideal type'; if the complexion of the impure type appears to be closer to a different regime type than originally argued, then sufficient grounds may exist to reallocate the nation state into another category.

Third, Bruff's (2011) critique of the varieties of capitalism literature focuses on the tendency to equate all forms of social life to key institutions. Rather, Bruff (2011) continues to assert, 'if all social practices embody conceptions about the world, then institutions have a distinctly capitalist character and thus privilege capital over labour on an everyday basis' (p 483). Bruff makes an important epistemological point – there is a danger that our attention is drawn to the institutional level when comparing societies' harm reduction systems at the expense of an understanding of the balance of forces within given societies that form the basis of these systems. Thus it is crucial that the development of ideal types provides a means to capture broader social practices, alongside detailing the forms that institutions take within these societies.

Noting these caveats, as well as the limitations of developing ideal types, the remainder of this section details the ways in which the models of harm production were constructed. Clearly, there is nothing new about creating models that capture aspects of capitalist society as a means to promote comparison. Therefore, the 'ideal types' presented here draw on existing models – as well as develop additional ones – that map different aspects of harm production within capitalist societies. While these models provide specific insights into distinct features of capitalist harm, using these 'ideal types' allows empirical analyses to explore 'co-variance' between these elements to begin to build understanding of the complex interplay of structural features (Schroeder, 2009). It is important to acknowledge that the harm production models presented are based on typologies developed for contrasting reasons that have very different epistemological approaches. This does not necessarily invalidate the combination of these models, although it is crucial that the specific insights offered by these models are highlighted, so that both the strengths and limitations of the lens they hold to capitalist formations can be understood.

The varying forms that the mode of production takes is addressed first. Numerous models have been generated from the 'varieties of capitalism' literature. While Hall and Soskice's classic model (2001) suggests two forms, the 'coordinated' market economy and the 'market economy', the regulatory approach pioneered by Boyer (2005) offers a more complex approach that has a greater resonance with other models used here. Boyer's writing, within the tradition of the Regulation school, views capitalism as an inherently unstable form, whereby accumulation regimes are given varying degrees of stability through a host of institutional arrangements. Thus, we gain insights into the form that the arrangements of the abstraction of surplus value take, as well as the patterns of wealth accumulation that form within national territories. In terms of harm production, we are able to begin to build knowledge of the severity and experience of economic exploitation and resulting harms – such as low pay, long working hours and so on – between social forms. In addition, through a focus on institutional characteristics, we can sketch the social arrangements that make either forms of capitalism relatively volatile or stable – thus the extent to which they are crisis-prone provides an important generative context from which harms can result from periods of recession, market crashes, the demise of speculative bubbles and so on.

Second, we draw on Esping-Andersen's (1990) seminal threefold model of welfare regimes and its subsequent critiques that offer potential insights into the social arrangements that either serve to mitigate or exacerbate the divisions and inequalities generated by modes of production. Esping-Andersen's concern is to understand the varying degrees of 'decommodifcation' that ensure the extent to which individuals are able to achieve their living standards independent of the market. From a social harm perspective, the extent to which decommodification can be achieved serves to reduce the incidence and intensity of harms, particularly in relation to harms such as poverty. While welfare regimes have clear harm reduction properties, their relationship to harm production is far more complex and contradictory than this, insofar as these systems also exist, in many instances, to maintain the conditions of accumulation and to underwrite the harmful relations of production in question, which has led many commentators to refer to the 'legitimatory' function of the welfare state (Gough, 1979). More specifically, the social arrangements that constitute these regimes provide a generative context – be it through minimal levels of state assistance, restrictive access to health and education services, or the stigma attached to the receipt of means-tested rather than universal benefits and services. These are fragile political arrangements based on hard-fought concessions; thus, the balance between the harm reduction capacities and the generative aspects of these systems are subject to constant political renewal, whereby social rights are either realised or undermined as regimes expand or contract – analyses must remain sensitive to these temporal shifts.

Third, Cavadino and Dignan's (2006) comparative models of penal policy have been developed as a means to capture the variance in prison populations, particularly through an investigation of the practices and ideologies of punishment. In doing so they offer a series of insights into the responses to criminal harms and the social arrangements that are either criminogenic – conditions that facilitate these harms – or conversely, that militate against these harms. Again, it should be noted that punishment and the relationship to criminal harms is complex. The subsequent analyses explores whether societies that use prison as an exclusionary tool are more or less likely to reduce criminal harms than countries that appear to have less punitive approaches. Moreover, it is important here that we note the synergies between harm reduction systems – in particular, between welfare and criminal justice systems – as well as varying forms of social solidarity. Underlying logics appear to underpin the connections between these systems. Thus, societies based on an individualist rather than a collectivist ethos will view the harms that result from the market, such as poverty or exclusion, to be largely due to personal failings; similarly, crime is constructed as the fault of free-willed individuals, which informs the punitive sensibilities of these societies. There is growing academic interest in this relationship, particularly in whether societies with more minimalist welfare states resort to the criminal justice system as a means to deal with the conflicts that result from the individualism and inequity of a capitalist society. Indeed, societies that are more individualised and unequal appear to provide criminogenic contexts, as they are likely to experience lower levels of social cohesion and increased marginalisation, therefore engendering greater doses of anomie and alienation from which increased criminal harms may result.

The final two elements that constitute the harm reduction model are not based on pre-existing models. Perhaps most surprisingly, there is not a comparative model of corporate regulation; however, this may be explained by the diversity of regulatory styles within nation states between systems of environmental protection, health and safety, financial services and so on – so one can expect less uniformity in approach within nation states. Yet, from the literature reviewed, it would appear that their remains sufficient uniformity within nation states to refer to the state as a unit of analysis, particularly in terms of prevailing attitudes towards enforcement of regulatory law surrounding corporate activities. With this in mind, the regulatory approaches developed here are derived from an amalgamation of the available comparative literature – which is admittedly thin – to form a set of ideal types within the harm reduction models presented in Table 3.1. There is certainly scope here for future research. Again, there are clear synergies between the regulatory styles adopted and the mode of production, insofar as both highlight contrasting aspects of the relationship between the state and capital, and the extent to which the state is willing to organise and intervene within the market to prevent the production of specific harms. Thus, what is in question here is not only the extent to which the state creates regulations that govern the operations of capital, but the willingness of the state and its regulatory agencies to enforce these rules. Regulatory zeal may be determined by the resources made available for these agencies and the number of inspectors they have at their disposal, to not only inspect, but also to ensure breaches of regulatory law are pursued; nevertheless, it is often persuasive free market ideologies that weaken the state's resolve – resulting in at best, 'compliance' approaches, and at worse, capital-led 'voluntary codes'.

Finally, inserted into the harm reduction model presented here is social solidarity. This is discussed within the 'welfare state regimes' and 'criminal justice regimes' literature in a dialectic fashion as being determined by and determining the shape these regimes take, yet social solidarity transcends specific aspects. In many respects, attitudes within society to harm determine the production of harms in the first instance, as well as our responses to the existence of harms in terms of harm reduction. Within the ideal types proposed in Table 3.1, it is suggested that societies differ in critical ways in relation to solidarity. Thus societies that are highly atomised will naturally demonstrate low levels of trust and cohesion, which, it is proposed, give rise to harm facilitative contexts, insofar as bonds with others within society are weaker, and therefore the restraining factors that limit propensity to harm are constantly undermined by the vague nature of these ties. This does not just apply to the anomie that is deployed to explain the anti-social acts of the marginalised, whereby formal opportunities to achieve the materialist goals of society are frustrated by unequal access to these opportunities, giving way to harmful responses (often criminal harms), but the harms that occur as result of the seemingly unlimited rewards offered to the powerful. Moreover, the social distance that develops within these societies as a result of inequality seemingly serve to legitimate participation in harm production, as our moral compulsion is restricted to ensuring our own individual interests at the expense of others. Conversely, it is proposed that the greater the levels of solidarity, trust and cohesion within a society, concern for others increases, which is therefore more likely to bring moral concerns into play for the consequence of one's actions beyond one's own self-interest – thus, reducing the production of harms.

In terms of harm reduction systems, it is proposed that these systems are more comprehensive within societies that have greater levels of solidarity. Thus, concern for others is likely to have a great impact on the form that harm reduction takes, insofar as societies with low levels of social solidarity are likely to demonstrate weaker collective responsibility for others. Therefore, highly atomised societies where individualised explanations of harm predominate are less likely to view harm as a product of social relations and consequently, a reflection of the shared responsibility for the form that society takes. Alternatively, it is proposed, then, that where high degrees of collective responsibility exist, greater populist support surrounds the mechanisms of harm reduction, due to the concern for the 'other'.

Table 3.1: Harm reduction regime types

	Regime type				
	Neoliberal	Liberal	Corporatist	Meso-corporatist	Social democratic
Mode of production	Societies undertake radical economic transformation through 'shock doctrine' policies that facilitate rapid economic liberalisation. Volatile and chaotic economic development. Dominated by oligarch interests resulting from highly competitive, unplanned economic development economies, as well as instances of 'primitive accumulation' via former public utilities. De-unionised workplaces, low levels of worker representation and wage bargaining. High level of integration into global financial markets. Open borders to global chains of production, goods, and capital	Short-term profit motive dominates economic decision making. Highly competitive economies, giving rise to monopoly. De-unionised workplaces, low levels of worker representation and wage bargaining, highly segmented labour market. Financial markets dominate economic decision making. High level of integration into global financial markets. State organises economic activity at the margins of the economy	Economic activity organised through public intervention. Tripartite structures govern the development and institutionalisation of regulations relating to employment, working hours and wages. State controls integration into global markets (tariffs, restrictions on financial flows)	Corporatism minus worker representation. Economic activity organised through state-corporate alliance. Relatively few, large companies with diverse outputs dominate. Companies demonstrate high levels of solidarity, characterised by wage compromise and synchronised pay awards. Competition intense within product markets. Competitiveness in global production to be achieved through technological and organisational innovation	Social partners negotiate the organisation of economic activity. High levels of worker representation, collective bargaining widespread. Monetary policy designed to achieve full employment, rather than competitiveness. Competitiveness in global production to be achieved through technological and organisational innovation

(continued)

Table 3.1: Harm reduction regime types (continued)

	Regime type				
	Neoliberal	Liberal	Corporatist	Meso-corporatist	Social democratic
Welfare	Minimal safety net provision – heavily means-tested social security systems. User fees imposed on education and healthcare. Large segments of welfare delivery through private sector companies	Residual systems targeted to address the needs of low-income households. Entitlement rules are heavily circumscribed and stigmatise recipients. Means-tested assistance or modest social insurance dominate provision. Modest benefits and limited services designed to encourage labour market participation. The market, voluntary organisations and family play key roles in welfare delivery	Social insurance schemes status-based, that follow occupational hierarchies. Broadly rights-based systems. Corporatist regimes are influenced by the church and therefore the traditional family unit plays a key role. When the family unit is unable to support its members, the state intervenes	Social insurance schemes status-based, that follow occupational hierarchies. Insurance benefits are modest and have strict eligibility criteria. Basic state provision is supplemented by an extensive range of corporate benefits, from health and pensions, to leisure and funeral services. Market and family dominate delivery of welfare	Universal rights-based system. State key mechanism for the delivery of welfare. Characterised by generous provision, particularly services that socialise costs of care, education etc. Full employment is pursued and crucial to system, with many policies designed to enhance human capital in pursuit of this goal

(continued)

Table 3.1: Harm reduction regime types (continued)

	Regime type				
	Neoliberal	Liberal	Corporatist	Meso-corporatist	Social democratic
Criminal justice	Heavily authoritarian in nature, state agents frequent and unfettered use of coercive and brutal force. Extrajudicial killings commonplace. Punishment characterised by exclusionary methods, including reliance on high rates of imprisonment as a mechanism for incapacitation. Crime is viewed as an act perpetrated by free, autonomous and rational actors	Penal ideology heavily influenced by law and order rhetoric, with punishment characterised by exclusionary methods including reliance on imprisonment as a mechanism for incapacitation. Crime is viewed as an act perpetrated by free, autonomous and rational actors. Therefore, punishment tends to be harsher, with these systems characterised by higher levels of imprisonment	Dominant penal ideology emphasises rehabilitation, punishment characterised by moderate imprisonment and diversionary policies for young offenders. Communitarian attitudes, mean that offenders are not viewed as isolated individuals but require socialisation, a shared responsibility of the community. Penal welfarism designed to improve opportunities for offenders and to reintegrate into society	Dominant penal ideology is 'apology-based restoration'. Low use of imprisonment, with emphasis placed on inclusionary community-based strategies. The weak sense of individuality and strong commitment to the collective are embraced by the criminal justice system. Emphasis on apology as mechanism for re-socialisation, punitive measures exist for those not willing to apologise.	Dominant penal ideology is one of welfarism and inclusion. Emphasis placed on collective responsibility for crimes occurring, partial rejection of free will of offender. Policy focus on addressing the social context of offending through social policies. Low imprisonment rates

(continued)

Table 3.1: Harm reduction regime types (continued)

	Regime type				
	Neoliberal	Liberal	Corporatist	Meso-corporatist	Social democratic
Regulation	Characterised by high degrees of voluntarism or self-regulation. Minimal levels of legal enforcement. Minimal funding/resources for regulatory agencies	Characterised by high degrees of voluntarism or self-regulation. Minimal levels of legal enforcement. Minimal funding/resources for regulatory agencies	Compliance tri-partite system, based on interest groups, corporate, state relations. Moderate levels of legal enforcement. Moderate levels funding/resources for regulatory agencies	A closed consensual 'compliance' model, based on corporate-state relations. Minimal levels of legal enforcement. Minimal funding/resources for regulatory agencies	Compliance tri-partite system, based on interest groups, corporate, state relations. High levels of legal enforcement. High degree of funding/resources for regulatory agencies
Social solidarity	Highly individualised societies, exhibiting low levels of trust and social cohesion, give rise to high levels of anomie and anti-social tendencies at all levels of society. Characterised by high levels of socio-economic inequality serve to exclude and marginalise large swathes of the population. Large concentrations of wealth held by few oligarchs and extracted by global capital. Weak collective responsibility for others	Highly individualised societies, exhibiting low levels of trust and social cohesion give rise to high levels of anomie and anti-social tendencies at all levels of society. Characterised by high levels of socio-economic inequality serve to exclude and marginalise subgroups of the population. Weak collective responsibility for others	Hierarchical societies based on occupational status and structures. Reliance on family unit to absorb and manage risks generated through the market. State intervention serves to reduce inequalities, but serious consequences, both material and stigma, for those with weak familial networks. Strong reciprocal obligations	Hierarchical societies based on occupational status and structures. Low income differentials. High levels of social solidarity marked by strong reciprocal obligations to familial networks, community and between employer and employee. Serious consequences for those who fall outside these relations	Solidaristic societies characterised by high degree of social citizenship that affords a high degree of protection against harmful aspects. Low levels of inequality and a strong commitment to inclusion. High degree of collective responsibility and concern for the 'other'

Allocating nation states to regime types

Having outlined the ideal harm reduction types, the next step is to match nation states to these hypothecated regimes. This is, of course, fraught with potential pitfalls. As identified earlier, some nation states will be a closer fit to these ideal types than others. Envisaging nation states as being located along a continuum, demonstrating contrasting adherence to harm reduction characteristics, allows analysis to comment on the extent to which nation states represent purer forms of these ideal types than others, and where they overlap with others. Therefore, it is important that when allocating nation states to ideal types we remain cognisant of the degree of fit between empirical case and the characteristics of the hypothecated regime type. The process of allocating nation states to regime types was guided by two methodological stages.

The first sought to draw on pre-existing models to assist with the designation of nation states to the regime types. As described above, Boyer's mode of production (2005), Esping Andersen's welfare regimes (1990) and Cavadino and Dignan's criminal justice systems (2006) have influenced the development of the harm reduction model presented here; each model allocates nation states to an ideal regime type. There is remarkable consistency between these different models in the selection of nation states as well as the categorisation of ideal types. While labels attached to regime types differ between these models, this tends to reflect a slippage of language rather than representing contrasting models of capitalist form – in other words, it would appear that these are cognate categories. The allocation undertaken in these models then forms the basis of the initial selections made in the harm reduction model in Table 3.2.

The existing models are extended here in the following ways. First, these models do not capture the development in capitalist modes that have emerged over the last 40 years. Most significantly, the focus in these models is on established 'advanced industrialised' nation states, and they fail to capture the transformation undertaken through the 'Washington Consensus' in lower and middle-income countries from which distinctly neoliberal forms arise. In many countries this transformation has occurred as a result of the leverage exerted through trade and loan agreements, such as the North American Free Trade Agreement (NAFTA), and international financial institutions, in particular The World Bank and IMF, that promoted a neoliberal restructuring ethos. More dramatically, for 'crisis' or 'transformation' states, 'shock doctrine' economic liberalisation served to overhaul

Table 3.2: Allocation of nation states to harm reduction regime

Comparative model	Neo-liberalism	Liberal	Corporatist	Meso-corporatist	Social democratic
Mode of production (Boyer, 2005, regulation theory)		*Market capitalism* UK/US/CA/ AUS/IRE/NZ	*State capitalism* AT/GER/BE/ NL/FR/IT/ESP/ POR	*Meso-corporatist capitalism* JP	*Social-partner capitalism* SWE/FIN/ DK/NOR
Welfare (Esping Andersen, 1999, welfare state regime)		*Liberal welfare state* UK/US/CA/ AUS/IRE/NZ	*Conservative welfare states* AT/GER/BE/ FR/IT/ESP/ POR (NL/JP ambiguous)	*East Asian fourth world* JP/KOR	*Social democratic welfare states* SWE/FIN/ DK/NOR
Criminal justice (Cavadino and Dignan, 2006, political economy and penality)	*Neo-liberalism* UK/US/ AUS/NZ		*Conservative corporatism* GER/FR/IT/NL	*Oriental corporatism* JP	*Social democratic* SWE/FIN
Harm reduction (proposed allocation)	*Neo-liberalism* CH/RU/ ME/TU	*Liberal* UK/US/CA/ AUS/IRE/NZ	*Northern corporatism* AT/GER/BE/ NL/FR/ ⟶ *Southern corporatism* IT/ESP/POR/GR ⟶ *Post-socialist corporatism* POL/CZ/SLR/ HU/ES/SL	*Meso-corporatism* JP/KOR	*Social democratic* SWE/FIN/ DK/NOR

an existing system and replace it with an 'off the peg' neoliberal formation. Thus, the harm reduction model presented here proposes to include a separate neoliberal form. Comparative data is available for four countries that fall within the remit of the neoliberal ideal type. Thus, Chile and the Russian Federation were societies radically transformed by the 'transplantation' of a neoliberal policy template and statecraft (Nesvetailova, 2005; Taylor, 2005; Klein, 2007), whereas Mexico and Turkey's path to neoliberalism was less abrupt, achieved through incremental pressure exerted through trade agreements and international lending (Soederberg, 2005).

Second, corporatism appears to present a series of challenges for existing classifications, and is the greatest point of variance between the approaches identified. It tends to be presented either as a single category, as per Esping-Andersen, or, according to Boyer and Cavadino and Dignan, it is divided into two, with the introduction of the East Asian corporatist forms as a distinct regime. It is worth noting that Esping Andersen's categorisation of East Asian, as well as Southern European nation states within a general corporatist category, drew a great deal of criticism in subsequent debates surrounding his classic work. Therefore, the harm reduction regimes presented here have categorised the corporatist nation states in the following ways.

The meso-corporatist regime has been designated as a distinct form of corporatist regime due to the cultural influence of Confucianism. The corporatism category is subdivided into three further groups – Northern European, Southern European and post-socialist – to acknowledge that the corporatist configuration differs markedly according to the very specific historical and cultural trajectories of these societies. Moreover, Southern European nation states, such as Italy, Portugal, Spain and Greece, have radically transformed state provision of social security, health and so on, as a result of austerity programmes in the wake of the credit crunch, that distinguish them from their Northern European counterparts. Similarly, the post-socialist societies' transformations from communism to capitalism demonstrate a specific historical trajectory, providing a distinct variation on the corporatist theme (Deacon, 2007).

The next methodological phase sought to empirically test the initial categorisation presented above. This was achieved through the selection of socioeconomic indicators that reflect, as far as possible, the different characteristics of the harm reduction models described earlier. In turn, this allowed a judgement to be made in relation to the match between nation states and their allocation to particular harm reduction regimes. A nation state's membership of a family type was assessed on the 'totality' of the specific social form in question, and by considering all aspects of harm reduction, rather than excluding nation states on the basis that singular aspects of harm reduction did not cohere with the ideal type. As suggested earlier, the ideal type becomes an analytical 'resource' that can be contrasted with the empirical reality of specific nation states, thus, where states map on to these ideal types and where they diverge are important points of analysis, as they may begin to illuminate the organisational features of societies that appear to reduce or increase specific harms.

Table 3.3 summarises the indicators that are used in the study to capture the varied aspects of the harm reduction models. These are predominantly drawn from OECD (Organisation for Economic

Table 3.3: Harm reduction indicators

Harm reduction indicator	Indicator description	Source	Year (indi-cator)
Trade union density	Trade union density corresponds to the ratio of wage and salary earners that are trade union members, divided by the total number of wage and salary earners	OECD	2008
Pensions spend	Public expenditure on pension cash benefits as a percentage of GDP	OECD	2009
Including Sup spend	Public expenditure on Income Support cash benefits for working-age population as a percentage of GDP	OECD	2009
Health spend	Public expenditure on health as a percentage of GDP	OECD	2009
Services spend	Public expenditure on social services (except health) as a percentage of GDP	OECD	2009
Education spend	Direct public expenditure on educational institutions plus public subsidies to households (which include subsidies for living costs) and other private entities, as a percentage of GDP	OECD	2006
Active labour market policies spend	Public expenditure on active labour market policies as a percentage of GDP	OECD	2010
UN rep rate	Net replacement rates as a proportion of average male earnings in first year of unemployment	OECD	2007
Pensions rep rate	Net replacement rates as a proportion of average earnings	OECD	2008
Child benefit	Cash benefits exclusively for families (e.g. child payments and allowances, parental leave benefits) as a percentage of GDP	OECD	2009
Child services	Services that are exclusively available for families (e.g. childcare support)	OECD	2009
Child support	Scores attributed to comparative worth of child	Bradshaw	2002
Social spend	Public expenditure on cash benefits and services (health, education, social services and active labour market policies spend) as a percentage of GDP	OECD	2009
Criminal justice spend	Public order and safety spending (police, courts and prison) as a percentage of GDP	OECD	2009
Prison rate	The basic indicator of the size of the prison population is each country is the number of people in prison (including pre-trial detainees and remand prisoners) per 100,000 of national population	World Prison Brief	2008/09
Employment regulation	Employment protection measure derived using synthetic indicators of the strictness of regulation relating to the costs of individual and collective dismissals and the use of temporary contracts	OECD	2008
Inequality	Gini coefficient based on equivalised household disposable income, after taxes and transfers	OECD	Late 2000s
Trust	Percentage of people expressing high level of trust in others	OECD	2008

Co-operation and Development) datasets, as these provide the most appropriate indicators to capture the aforementioned features of the models, as well as provide the most comprehensive coverage for 31 nation states. However, there are a number of limitations in relation to this data that must be noted. First, this exercise is obviously subject to the availability of appropriate indicators that map on to the various aspects described in the ideal types, and that also provide consistent coverage for all nation states. Coverage for different harm reduction aspects vary considerably. Mode of production has a single indicator, 'trade union density', that acts as a proxy for industrial relations. Other indicators, such as measures for 'collective bargaining' and 'worker representation', were considered, yet the available indicators were dated and coverage limited. Numerous contextual economic indicators exist that offer insights into the public/private composition of national economies, as well as the extent to which they are integrated into global markets. However, these were not included as they are too indirect as measures to understand the determining impacts on the production of specific harms. Welfare indicators demonstrate the greatest level of coverage, with expenditure and generosity indicators available for virtually all areas of social policy, as well as comprehensive coverage for nation states – with the exception of the neoliberal regime. One significant gap is the absence of indicators that capture the extent of means-tested benefits and services that demonstrate the balance between residualism and universalism in different systems. Criminal justice has two indicators, 'criminal justice spend' and 'prison rates', which demonstrate reasonable coverage across the regimes – with the exception of 'criminal justice spend' for the neoliberal regime. While these indicators acts as proxies for the values that inform criminal justice systems, measures of average sentence length would better illuminate the contrasting levels of punitiveness in contrasting societies. Social solidarity has two indicators, 'inequality' and 'trust', that demonstrate comprehensive coverage across the regimes and capture significant aspects of this category. An omission from this category is an indicator that captures measures of societal empathy, which offers insight into the collective responsibility for others. Regulation has a single indicator, 'employment regulatory burden', that provides a measure for labour market regulation. This category has the poorest coverage in the absence of comparative indicators for regulatory spend, numbers of inspectors or regulatory activities (sanctions and prosecutions), and there is therefore less that can be inferred from the regime types in relation to particular harms.

The use of spending data to measure forms of harm reduction must be treated with some caution. In particular, in relation to welfare regimes, there is a considerable amount of comparative data on welfare expenditure, yet the extent to which this is instructive in terms of harm reduction is questionable. In a universalist system, welfare spending is more likely to go directly to the benefits or services that individuals receive, whereas in a selective system, spending reflects more the administration of means testing and the rationing of services. While different regimes may prima facie have similar expenditure levels, this masks whether the regimes serve to protect or, through the denial of support, produce harms. Therefore, spending data must always be supplemented by alternative indicators that allow an examination of the extent to which a system offers protection. In the case of welfare regimes, expenditure data presented alongside other indicators reflects the generosity of the system and the degree to which payments are means tested.

The indicators used to represent harm reduction/production features have been clearly distinguished from harm indicators in this analysis. However, this separation is not always immediately obvious; there are two indicators used here that equally could also be viewed as harms. Thus, inequality and imprisonment could be viewed as harms and are often referred to as being harmful. The difficulty is that both phenomena are instances of harm, as well as providing the contexts through which harms are generated. They are considered here as aspects of harm reduction/production, insofar as they are primarily the contexts for a number of different harms that the book examines.

From Tables 3.4 and 3.5, it is possible to identify commonalities between the families of nation states allocated to the ideal types. It is also possible to identify points of divergence within these families. None of these are necessarily fatal, but it is important that they are noted as they may explain variations in the contrasting levels of harm experienced within regime types. Similarly, the points where nation states from different regime types appear to overlap and coalesce again require analytical scrutiny, insofar as the boundaries of these ideal types may not be as clearly delineated as they appear to be in the rather stylised hypothecated versions. We now take each regime in turn.

As a family of nation states, the social democratic regime, according to the indicators in Table 3.4, demonstrate a high degree of consistency between these states in relation to the selected harm reduction indicators. Thus, this regime is very much a distinct social form, as it is clearly distinguishable from the other regimes in relation to a number of aspects: the role of trade unions, the generosity of its

Table 3.4: Harm reduction regimes and harm reduction indicators: neoliberal, liberal and social democratic

	Neoliberal					Liberal							Social democratic				
	RU	CH	ME	TU	Average	AU	CA	IRE	NZ	UK	US	Average	DE	FI	NO	SW	Average
Mode of production																	
Trade union density	15	13.3		5.9	11.4	18.2	29.2	32.2	20.6	27.1	11.9	23.2	67.6	67.5	53.3	68.5	64.2
Welfare state																	
Pensions spend		1.9	1	0.5	1.1	4.6	5.4	8.7	5.9	5.6	2.6	5.0	7.9	7.1	6.3	5.5	6.7
UN spend		3.6	1.7	6.8	4.0	3	4.5	5.1	4.7	6.2	6.8	5.1	6.1	9.9	5.4	8.2	7.4
Health spend		3.7	3.1	5.4	4.1	6.2	8	7.1	8.3	8.1	8.3	7.7	7.7	6.8	6.2	7.3	7
Services spend		1.9	2.4	0.1	1.5	3.3	0.9	1.6	2	1.1	1.1	2.1	6.9	4.7	5	7.7	6.1
Education spend	3.9	3.4	4.8	2.9	3.8	4.6	5.1	4.9	6	5.5	5.5	5.3	8	6.1	6.6	6.8	6.9
Active labour market policies spend		0.1	0			0.3	0.3	1	0.3	0.3	0.1	0.4	2.1	1.1	0.8	1.1	1.4
UN replacement rate	75			46		42	52	77	56	62	36	54	73	69	70	65	69
Pensions replacement rate		65	50	98	72	66	62	41	50	48	53	53	95	65	62	57	70
Child benefit		0.74	4			1.94	1.12	3.26	2.47	2.46	0.11	1.9	1.63	1.67	1.42	1.58	1.6
Child services		0.74	7			1.84	0.23	0.82	1.08	1.38	0.84	1.0	2.27	1.62	1.79	2.17	2.0
Child support						123	40	91	-5	142	123		140	191	136	153	
Social spending	12	11.3	8.2	12.8	11.1	17.8	19.2	23.6	21.2	24.1	19.2	20.9	30.2	29.4	23.3	29.8	28.2
Criminal justice																	
Criminal justice spend									2	2.8	2.3	2.4	1.2	1.5	1	1.4	1.3
Prison rate	624	317	208	155	326	129	116	85	195	153	760	240	63	67	70	74	68.5
Regulation																	
Employment regulation		1.93	3.23	3.46	2.87	1.38	1.02	1.39	1.16	1.09	0.85	1.15	1.91	2.29	2.65	2.06	2.23
Social solidarity																	
Inequality	0.401	0.494	0.476	0.409	0.445	0.336	0.324	0.293	0.33	0.342	0.378	0.33	0.248	0.259	0.25	0.259	0.254
Trust	28.3	13.4	26.1	23.5	22.8	63.9	55.8		69.1	68.9	48.7	61.3	88.8	85.5	88.3	83.7	85.8

Table 3.5: Harm reduction regimes and harm reduction indicators: southern, post-socialist, northern and meso-corporatist

	Southern corporatist					Post-socialist corporatist							Northern corporatist						Meso corporatist		
	IT	GR	PO	SP	Aver-age	CZ	ES	HU	POL	SLR	SL	Aver-age	AT	BE	FR	GER	NL	Aver-age	JP	KOR	Aver-age
Mode of production																					
Trade union density	33.4	24.0	20.5	15.0	19.5	17.3	8.1	16.8	15	17.2	25.6	16.7	29.1	51.9	7.6	19.1	18.8	25.3	18.2	10.3	14.3
Welfare state																					
Pensions spend	3.4	2.6	4.6	6.0	4.2	4.4	5.7	5.7	3.4	4.3	3.6	4.5	5.8	8.1	5.2	4.4	6.3	6.0	2.2	1.3	1.8
UN spend	15.4	13	12.3	9.3	12.5	8.3	7.9	9.9	11.8	7	10.9	9.3	8.1	10	13.7	11.3	5.1	9.6	10.2	2.1	6.2
Health spend	7.4	6.5	7.2	7	7	6.7	5.2	5.1	5.2	6	6.8	5.8	5.2	8.1	9	8.6	7.9	7.8	7.1	4	5.8
Services spend	1.1	1.5	0.7	2	1.3	1.1	1	2.7	0.6	1.2	1	1.3	1.7	2.1	3.3	2.5	2.7	2.5	2.4	1.5	2
Education spend	4.7		5.3	4.3	4.8	4.4	4.8	5.4	5.3	3.8	5.7	4.9	5.4	6	5.6	4.4	5.5	5.4	3.5	4.5	4
Active labour market policies spend	0.4		0.7	0.9	0.7	0.3	0.2	0.4	0.4	0.3	0.4	0.3	0.8	1.5	1.1	0.9	1.2	1.1	0.3	0.4	0.35
UN replacement rate	76	33	79	69	64	33	63	48	42	32		38.8	69	64	58	59	73	65	75	39	57
Pensions replacement rate	37	110	66	85	75	73		100	68	73	90	77.8	90	66	61	58	103	76	41	52	47
Child benefit	0.78	1.02	1.03	0.67	0.88	1.24	2.18	2.42	0.75	1.57	0.76	1.5	2.34	1.77	1.44	1.16	0.78	1.50	0.51	0.04	0.28
Child services	0.8	0.4	0.47	0.85	0.63	0.6	0.44	1.16	0.33	0.44	0.53	0.6	0.57	1.04	1.76	0.89	0.93	1.03	0.45	0.77	0.61
Child support	28	-59	-15	-15									266	142	162	152	-34		-26		
Social spending	27.8	23.6	25.6	26.0	25.8	20.7	20	23.9	21.5	18.7	22.6	21.2	29.1	29.7	32.1	27.8	23.2	28.4	22.4	9.4	15.9
Criminal justice																					
Criminal justice spend	2	1.9	2.2	2.1	2.1	2.2	2.4	2	2	3.6	1.7	2.3	1.6	1.9	1.3	1.7	2	1.7	1.5	1.4	1.5
Prison rate	97	109	104	164	119	209	273	152	225	151	65	179	99	93	96	90	100	96	63	97	80
Regulation																					
Employment regulation	2.58	2.97	3.05	3.11	2.93	2.32		2.11	2.41	2.13	2.76	2.35	2.41	2.61	3	2.63	2.23	2.58	1.73	2.13	1.93
Social solidarity																					
Inequality	0.337	0.307	0.353	0.317	0.329	0.256	0.315	0.272	0.305	0.257	0.236	0.274	0.261	0.259	0.293	0.295	0.294	0.280	0.329	0.314	0.322
Trust		40.4	38.1	61.9	46.8	55.7	72.1	46.8	47.4	47	52.9	53.7	61.8	68.6	55.8	61.1	79.7	65.4	60.7	46.2	53.5

welfare regimes, and in particular, social services, the limited role of punishment and the high levels of social solidarity. In stark contrast, the meso-corporatist regime is the most problematic, insofar as there appears to be considerable disparity between Japan and South Korea in notable aspects of harm reduction, such as welfare expenditure and generosity and trade union density. However, despite these disparities, the regime does demonstrate some form of coherence, high levels of inequality and low levels of punishment. For this reason the regime is included, yet it is acknowledged that further research and data is required to build more nation states into this family.

The corporatist regime, as described above in Table 3.5, is further subdivided into the northern, southern and post-socialist corporatist regimes. Each family of nation states demonstrates a high degree of coherence between member states. The difference between these regimes appears to be graduated – insofar as the post-socialist corporatist appears to demonstrate lower levels of harm reduction through to the northern corporatist that has a greater degree of harm reduction that gravitates toward the social democratic regime. There are notable points of difference – the southern corporatist tends to gravitate towards the characteristics displayed by liberal regimes, in relation to criminal justice, inequality and trade union density; likewise, the post-socialist corporatist regime in terms of criminal justice, overall social spend and trade union density.

The nation states within the liberal regime demonstrate conformity to low welfare spend/generosity and punitive criminal justice systems; higher levels of socioeconomic inequality; and low levels of employment regulation relative to the northern corporatist and social democratic regimes. However, what is striking about this family of nations is the degree to which the US diverges from other nation states, particularly in terms of the low levels of trade union density, markedly lower levels of service spend, child benefit and child services spend, low levels of employment regulation and high levels of imprisonment rates. As noted in relation to the corporatist regimes, both the post-socialist and southern corporatist regimes overlap in particular aspects with the less extreme nation states of the liberal regime. The neoliberal regime demonstrates similar characteristics to the liberal regime – low social spend/punitive criminal justice systems and low levels of social solidarity – yet these nation states are qualitatively distinct to the liberal regime insofar as the indicators demonstrate dramatically lower rates of social expenditure, higher imprisonment rates and socioeconomic inequality.

Harmful associations: regime types and harm indicators

Harms were selected principally because they could be defined as such using the definition outlined in Chapter Two. Thus the harms included in the analyses in Chapters Four and Five met a two-stage criteria: (i) they could be demonstrated empirically to either result in 'disablement' or 'impediment' to successful human action or participation; or (ii) that prima facie these events result from 'preventable' social circumstances, insofar as these conditions are 'alterable' social structures, policies etc. Each harm is discussed in relation to these criteria in Chapters Four and Five – with an obvious exception for those physical harms that result in death, a discussion of the 'impediment' to successful action that the harm presents is omitted for obvious reasons. The harm indicators selected are summarised in Table 3.6.

It should be noted that the selection of harm indicators was naturally limited to the availability of reliable comparative data. This certainly restricted the harms that could be included in these analyses in the following ways. While reasonable coverage of the facets of physical and autonomy harm exists in the indicators presented, mental health and relational harms proved to be more problematic. Mental health harms that could be most directly related to social determinants, such as anxiety and depression, demonstrated uneven coverage across the regimes, with too many missing cases. Relational harms, by their very nature, present specific challenges for comparative study, particularly the harms of misrecognition that do not easily translate across cultural contexts. Other harm indicators fall foul of inconsistencies in data collection between nation states; in particular, workplace deaths and injuries indicators are created using very different methodologies that frustrate meaningful comparison among the OECD nations to be drawn. For other harm indicators, for example, deaths caused by air pollution, there are no corresponding harm reduction indicators available, such as regulatory spend or regulatory activities, or, for that matter, a developed comparative literature that could explain the patterns in these harms. Finally, the comparisons between criminal and non-criminal harms are restricted to the use of homicide as a proxy for intentional harms and a comparator to non-intentional physical harms – due to the varied definitions and recording practices for crimes that again, frustrates comparative analysis.

The empirical chapters that follow seek to explore the variance of harms across regimes, as well as to begin to understand the reasons for the noted differences between these regimes. The analysis is based on evidence of statistical association, and is overlaid with the findings of

Table 3.6: Harm indicators

Harm	Indicator	Indicator description	Source	Year
Physical/mental health				
Intentional killing	Homicide rates per 100,000	Intentional homicide is defined as unlawful death purposefully inflicted on a person by another person	UNODC	2010
Infant mortality	Infant deaths per 1,000 live births	Infant mortality rate is based on the number of infants dying before reaching one year of age	OECD	2008
Obesity	Obese population, self-reported, percentage of total population	Obesity rates are self-reported through estimates of height and weight from population-based health interview surveys. The indicator is derived from this data using the BMI	OECD	2010 (or nearest year)
Suicide	Intentional self-harm, deaths per 100 000 population	Mortality rates are based on numbers of deaths registered in a country in a year divided by the size of the corresponding population. The classification of a death as suicide is based on reporting via death certificates	OECD	2010 (or nearest year)
Road traffic deaths	Transport accident mortality rates per 100,000 population	Mortality rates are based on numbers of deaths registered in a country in a year divided by the size of the corresponding population. The classification of a death as a transport fatality is based on the International Classification of Diseases ICD10 codes V01-V89 described as 'land-based transport accidents'	OECD	2009 (or nearest year)
Autonomy				
Relative poverty	Percentage of people with an income below 60% of median income	Percentage of people with an income below 60% of median income. Data are based on equivalised household disposable income, after taxes and transfers.	OECD	2008 (or nearest year)
Child poverty	Percentage of households with children whose income is below 50% of median income	Percentage of households with children whose income is below 50% of median income. Data are based on equivalised household disposable income, after taxes and transfers.	OECD	2008

(continued)

Table 3.6: Harm indicators (continued)

Harm	Indicator	Indicator description	Source	Year
Autonomy (continued)				
Long working hours	Percentage of workforce average working week 40+ hours	Percentage of workforce average working week 40+ hours. Estimates of the hours actually worked are based on national labour force surveys in most countries, while others use establishment surveys, administrative records or a combination of sources. Actual hours worked include regular work hours of full-time and part-time workers, overtime (paid and unpaid), hours worked in additional jobs, and time not worked because of public holidays, annual paid leave, illness, maternity and parental leave, strikes and labour disputes, bad weather, economic conditions and several other minor reasons.	OECD	2011
NEETs	Percentage of 15 to 19-year-olds not in education, employment or training	Percentage of 15- to 19-year-olds not in education, employment or training	OECD	2011
Relational				
Social isolation	Percentage of population that see family once a year or never	Percentage of population that see family once a year or never	EU-SILC	2005

the existing empirical literature that serve to contextualise and lend meaning to the associations presented. The remainder of this section describes in greater detail the statistical methods used in the book, and considers the implications of this approach.

Primarily, comparisons across regimes were conducted and reported in the following empirical chapters, with associations examined between the seven regimes introduced in this chapter and the identified harms. Analysis of variance (ANOVA) has been used to explore differences between the regimes. The p value generated by an ANOVA can be interpreted as the probability of observing the mean values in each regime if the difference between any two regime means is actually zero, that is, if the mean rate of a harm is the same in each of the seven regimes. For example, in Chapter Four, the first harm considered is intentional killing, and Table 4.1 reports the mean rate per 100,000 for each of the seven regimes. The corresponding ANOVA generates a p value of 0.002. This infers that there is only a 0.2 per cent chance of observing the means in Table 4.1 if, in fact, the seven true regime means are all identical. In other words, there is strong evidence that there is a difference between the regimes.

This p value alone, however, does not tell us exactly where the differences lie, although assumptions can be made by looking at the individual means for the regime. In Table 4.1, for example, it is quite likely that there is an important difference between regime 1, the neoliberal regime, and all other regimes, but are any of the other differences between regimes large enough to be unlikely to have occurred by chance? An ANOVA also produces 95 per cent confidence intervals around the observed difference between two regime means. A 95 per cent confidence interval gives us a range of values around an observed estimate that we can be 95 per cent confident that the true value lies within. Only differences between regimes that have been demonstrated to be unlikely to be due to chance have been reported.

Alongside the variance between regimes, Chapters Four and Five present scatter plots that consider the associations between specific harms and selected harm reduction indicators presented above. Each point on a plot represents an individual country, and the value of the exposure for that country is shown on the x-axis (horizontal) at the bottom of the graph and the outcome on the y-axis (vertical) at the left-hand side of the graph. In addition, a regression line is generated for each graph that represents the line of best fit between the harms and the harm reduction indicator. A flat line demonstrates that, as the exposure increases across countries (from left to right along the x-axis), the rate of harm does not, on average, change. An upward slope, on the other hand, suggests that as exposure increases, so does the rate of harm, and the steeper the slope, the greater the impact of increasing exposure. Finally, a downward slope demonstrates that as exposure increases, there is a decrease in the rate of harm. When a regression line is generated, a corresponding p value is also reported, which tells us the probability of observing the slope we have if, in actual fact, the regression line is flat – that is, that there is no association between the two variables. For each graph, the p value relating to the regression line is reported, but graphs have only been presented where the pattern is unlikely to have occurred by chance (where $p<0.05$). If the points representing the different countries are all close to the regression line, this demonstrates that the exposure is a strong predictor of the outcome. If the scatter is wide, then while the exposure may partially explain the outcome, there are likely to be other factors that also determine the rate of harm. A next step beyond this book would be to consider multiple regression that adjusts for the impact of other factors, but the number of countries available for analyses in this book are too few for such analyses to be meaningful.

Many of the harms presented in Chapters Four and Five have a normal distribution – that is, a symmetrical distribution about the mean where there are as many countries with rates above the mean as there are below – and the data is therefore summarised well by the mean. Some of the harms are, however, positively skewed (where there are more countries with rates of harm greater than the mean than there are with rates less than the mean). In this situation a better average measure to summarise the data is the median rather than the mean, and so for these variables, the medians have also been reported in the tables relating to regimes. In such circumstances the assumptions underlying the ANOVA may also be invalid. Transforming the data using a log transformation has the effect of stretching the data with lower values and squashing the data with higher values, resulting in more normally distributed data. Therefore, for positively skewed harms, the p values generated from ANOVAs and the examination of confidence intervals were based on the log-transformed data.

When producing a graph, as those described earlier, if one or both of the variables is heavily positively skewed, many of the countries will appear to clump together, which makes the individual countries hard to see on the graph. Using log-transformed data aids interpretation of such plots. While this can make the actual values on the graphs hard to interpret, the regression line can still be interpreted as evidence of a positive or negative association, or as no evidence of an association. Scatter plots considering harms with positively skewed distributions are presented on the log scale. All *p* values are reported to 3 decimal places or as $p<0.001$ or $p<0.0001$ as appropriate.

It remains to be said that the 'harmful associations' that are presented here are exactly that, associations, not causal explanations. It is hoped that the analyses presented arrive at a point where further refined hypotheses may be generated. Moreover, future analyses will be better placed to consider the impact of a wider range of societal factors on harm production – and thus are equipped to avoid accusations of confounding and 'ecological fallacy'. Nevertheless, with these contingencies in mind, the associations that are presented here are very persuasive; there is a weight of evidence that demonstrates some of the key determinants that appear to make some societies more harmful than others.

Conclusion

This chapter has built towards proposing a series of *harm hypotheses* to be explored in the remainder of the book. The aim of this chapter has been to present a series of theoretical arguments in relation to capitalist harm that capture the universal nature of this harm, as well as the aspects of the variety of capitalist form that determine the levels of harm that specific populations are exposed to. In respect of the former, it is empirically difficult to substantiate that alternative modes of organisation are less harmful forms – with few exceptions, such alternatives are currently not available for comparison. However, as the chapter has argued, it is possible to develop stylised models of varieties of capitalist form, and to test empirically the contrasting levels of harm experienced in these societies. Thus, the chapter has sought to move from rhetorical assertion to a position where these claims may be tested, so that at the very least, the levels of harm that vary between societies may be evaluated, and in so doing, we may understand the ways, to varying degrees, that particular harms are 'designed into' and 'designed out of' specific societies.

The chapter has presented seven distinct regimes that demonstrate contrasting harm reduction features. From this position it is possible to begin to speculate over which regimes could be the most successful in terms of 'designing out' harms from the social fabric of their respective societies. Indeed, the chapter concludes by proposing a 'harm hypothesis' that arranges the regimes into a continuum, ranging from the least harmful capitalist form to the most harmful. This is based on two assumptions. First, those societies that are able to ameliorate the most harmful elements of capitalism will prove to be the least harmful forms. Thus, the degree of exploitation involved in the extraction of surplus value varies according to the levels of worker representation and willingness of states to regulate this relation. Similarly, the generative contexts of harm will differ according to the extent to which social relations are 'decommodified' – in other words, the extent to which human life and flourishing are protected and valued within societies. Moreover, the more stable and less crisis-prone specific varieties of capitalist form are, the less harmful societies are. Second, as this chapter has argued, neoliberalism has sought to restore conditions of wealth accumulation that existed prior to an era of 'embedded liberalism', with various neoliberal projects seeking to dismantle aspects of harm reduction systems. As has been argued, neoliberalism has taken many forms, and its impacts are uneven, with some regimes better placed to resist and some more appropriate locations to facilitate its development.

To return to the notion of the continuum, drawing on the empirical indicators presented, it is proposed that the regimes that demonstrate the greatest levels of harm would be the neoliberal regime, followed by the liberal regime. The middle of the continuum consists of the post-socialist, southern and meso-corporatist regimes, with the northern corporatist and social democratic regimes demonstrating the least harmful societies. The following chapters explore these claims through the analysis of selected harms.

FOUR

Harm reduction regimes and the production of physical harm

This chapter focuses on the form that physical harms take within different capitalist societies. The analysis provided contrasts different forms of physical harm, from those that are viewed as resulting from individual intentional acts, such as homicide, or those that occur as result of 'biological' factors or accidents. Data provided demonstrate that intentional harms form a small part of the events that actually cause us physical injury – particularly when one compares homicide to the harms presented here, such as obesity, infant mortality and road traffic injuries. Indeed, what many of us would consider to be 'criminal events' appear to constitute only the 'tip' of the 'harm iceberg'. However, common sense often dictates that the harms that constitute the large proportion of these injurious events are determined by natural forces that, it is argued, lie beyond societal control. The analyses presented in this chapter seek to challenge the notion of a 'natural rate' for these harms insofar as each harm can be demonstrated to result from alterable social conditions, and thus, if specific societies were organised differently, it is likely that these harms would be significantly reduced.

The chapter explores the notion of 'preventable harm' through contrasting levels of physical harm between different varieties of capitalist state. These differences are explained through the lens of social organisation – the arrangements, policies and relations that constitute different societies. Moreover, the chapter provides, where possible within the constraints of the available data, analyses that seek to identify factors that serve to understand why some societies have greater levels of harm than others, thus offering insights into the factors that would appear to protect us from specific physical harms and those that seem to produce greater levels of harm.

Homicide

Homicide may appear to be an odd place to commence a social harm analysis. To begin with, in most capitalist societies murder rates are low and remain stable at the aggregate level. It is therefore highly unlikely any of us will be a homicide victim, or, for that matter, know someone whose life is ended as a result of homicide. Moreover, homicide is, in many respects, the quintessential individual level harm, most commonly viewed as an act of interpersonal violence resulting from intentional acts, and does not obviously fall into the remit of structural harms. Yet, as Dorling (2004, p 179) observes:

> The story behind the thousands of murder stories is more a testament to our shared inhumanity than a thriller. Murder, behind the headlines is the story of the connected consequences to our collective actions. Murder, despite being the rarest of crimes, tells us in the round a great deal about the millions of who will never be even remotely connected to such a death directly.

Rather than a set of random individual events, Dorling (2004, p 191) reminds us that 'murder is a social marker', which tells us as much about the state of our societies as it does about the individuals involved. As the analysis presented in this section will testify, homicide is an expression of a number of societal features.

From the data presented here, it is apparent that murder rates are low, and relatively little difference exists between the rates of many nations states. That said, there are countries where the murder rate is notably higher, that is, <2 per 100,000, in particular in the case of Mexico (23.7), Russian Federation (10.2), the US (4.8) and Estonia (5.2). These are significant differences, and the analysis presented here seeks to understand the reasons for these rates. As one would expect, then, the differences between regime type are less stark than for other harms; however, there are some notable forms of variance. It would appear prima facie that those countries that follow neoliberal orthodoxy more vehemently would appear to have higher rates of murder. This observation is supported, to some extent, when one examines the murder rate according to regime type (see Table 4.1).

An ANOVA of the rate of intentional killings (log scale) on regime demonstrated evidence of a difference between regimes unlikely to be due to chance ($p=0.002$). The mean rate within the neoliberal regime was significantly higher than that of all other regimes. There was no evidence of any difference between the other regimes that could not be explained by chance, all with overlapping confidence intervals.

With such small numbers of countries per regime, and some countries demonstrating higher murder rates than their regime mean,

Table 4.1: Intentional killing by regime

Regime	Intentional killing, mean rate per 100,000 (SD)	Median (range)	Number obs
1 Neoliberal	10.23 (9.52)	6.95 (3.3–23.7)	4
2 Liberal	1.82 (1.48)	1.20 (1.0–4.8)	6
3 Post-socialist corporatist	1.92 (1.64)	1.40 (0.7–5.2)	6
4 Southern corporatist	1.13 (0.30)	1.10 (0.8–1.5)	4
5 Meso-corporatist	1.50 (1.56)	1.50 (0.4–2.6)	2
6 Northern corporatist	1.06 (0.42)	1.10 (0.6–1.7)	5
7 Social democratic	1.18 (0.70)	0.95 (0.6–2.2)	4

in particular, Finland, Korea and the US, it is important to analyse individual nation state rates in relation to a number of structural features. The starting point for the analysis is the impact of social solidarity on murder rates – a factor that has been well documented within the existing criminological literature. In particular, numerous studies demonstrate the impact of inequality on murder rates, suggesting that intentional killing rates increase the more unequal a society is – and the analysis here appears to support this contention (Blau and Blau, 1982; Jacobs and Richardson, 2008; Pridemore, 2010; Wilkinson and Pickett, 2010).

Figure 4.1 demonstrates a significant association between murder rates (log scale) and inequality ($p<0.0001$). This would appear to lend credence to the notion that meritocratic societies that place significant emphasis on the material rewards associated with particular achievements promote high levels of interpersonal conflict when formal opportunities for social mobility are frustrated (Jacobs and Richardson, 2008). For Wilkinson and Pickett (2010), feelings of shame and humiliation are more acutely felt within markedly unequal societies – the degradation of identity serves as a catalyst for violence. Thus, while status in hierarchical market societies is predominantly determined by material possessions and our ability to consume, conversely, more people are deprived of the opportunity to obtain markers of status and social success. Unsurprisingly, given the findings in relation to inequality, trust ($p=0.002$) also appears to be strongly associated with murder rates (log scale). Thus, societies that demonstrate high levels of trust appear to have lower murder rates, and vice versa. Again this appears to resonate with the findings of previous studies; Lederman et al (2002) suggest that evidence of high levels of trust between members of a community or neighbourhood can serve to prevent violent crime.

Figure 4.1: Intentional killing/inequality

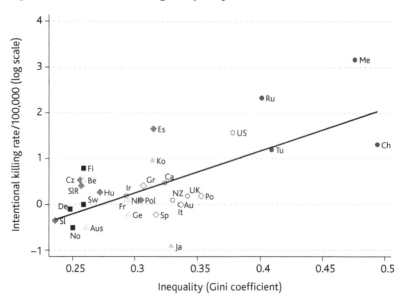

Given the interrelationship between fragmentation that occurs within ostensibly market societies and the low levels of social solidarity that characterise them, it follows that social expenditure on both benefits and services may serve to reduce homicide rates. A strong association was identified between social expenditure ($p<0.0001$) and homicide rates. Figure 4.2 demonstrates that the higher the aggregate social expenditure, the lower the murder rates experienced in nation states.

This serves to support a growing evidence base that has explored the relationship between murder rates and the impacts of social expenditure. Pridemore's review of homicide studies suggests, 'an association between decommodification and homicide rates, or that the effects of inequality on homicide are buffered in nations with higher levels of decommodification' (2010, p 764). Savolainen's analysis adds to this claim, when he concludes that nation states with generous social expenditure appear to be 'immune to the detrimental effects of economic inequality' due to the 'very small or nonexistent underclass population' (2000, p 1037). In other words, generous social expenditure appears to reduce the size of economically marginalised populations that are more likely to be susceptible to the effects of anomie. Messner and Rosenfield (1997) argue that societies dominated by the market to the detriment of social institutions, such as social security systems, schools and families, provide 'fertile soil for the

Figure 4.2: Intentional killing/social expenditure

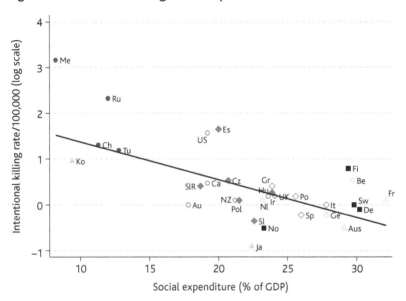

growth of anomie' as the role of these institutions in many societies is to 'bear the primary responsibility for cultivating respect for social norms' (p 1397).

Interestingly, in relation to the neoliberal project, which advocates a strong authoritarian 'nightwatchman' state, manifested in the extension of the penal complex and criminal justice system, while seeking to 'roll back' forms of the social state with its decommodification impact, nation states exhibiting facets of the strong state appear to have higher murder rates. Figures 4.3 and 4.4 demonstrate that higher nation states with higher imprisonment rates and criminal justice spend do not appear to 'buffer' nations against high murder rates.

One interpretation of these associations may suggest that this expenditure and rates of imprisonment are an expression of more violent societies that naturally have higher levels of homicide, and, therefore, are reflective of underlying trends in crime (Spelman, 2005). This 'logical leap' is deeply contestable; alternative explanations suggest that imprisonment rates are an artefact of broader patterns of inequality and declining social expenditure, as well as harsh sentencing regimen (Beckett and Western, 2001; Ouimet, 2012). Indeed, the 'strong state', with a reliance on the high use of imprisonment, is an ineffective crime control mechanism. Studies estimate the use of imprisonment in the US during the 1990s resulted in a 6 per cent fall (of a 33 per cent total drop) in violent crime; similarly in the UK, increased

Figure 4.3: Intentional killing/criminal justice spend

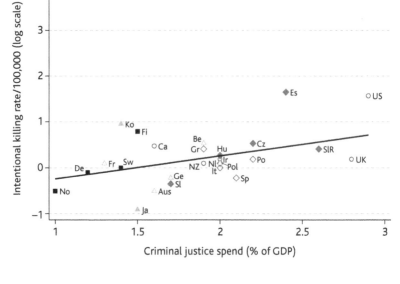

Figure 4.4: Intentional killing/imprisonment rates

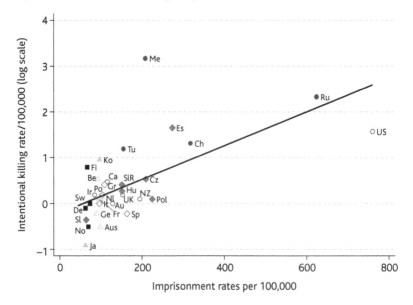

use of imprisonment in the late 1990s and early 2000s resulted in a 5 per cent decrease in the crime rate (Carter, 2003; Blumstein and Wallman, 2005). Thus, it would appear more likely that public safety in relation to homicide is enhanced by societies that have higher levels of solidarity and decommodification, rather than high levels of criminal justice spend and expansive penal systems.

Suicide

Suicide, like homicide, may appear to be an exclusively autonomous act, yet social science has long considered suicide to be an expression of societal dysfunction, with these acts situated within societal processes such as anomie, marginalisation and abrupt socioeconomic upheaval. Therefore suicide can be viewed as resulting from the habitual forms of marginalisation engrained within capitalist society, but we can also expect the volatility of these societies through various crises to generate peaks within suicide rates. While suicide claimed almost 150,000 lives in OECD countries in 2010, and it is ranked as one of the top 10 causes of death in the developed world, it should be noted that the long-term suicide trends in many advanced capitalist societies demonstrate a downward trajectory (OECD, 2011). Milner et al (2012) argue that this downward trend may, in part, be explained by rising levels of related health expenditure from 1980-2006 across OECD countries, speculating that this expenditure may have translated into the availability of mental health services, although this progress may now be reversed by the consequences of the credit crunch and austerity programmes currently underway in a number of nation states (Stuckler et al, 2009). For example, the first empirical study to examine suicide rates in Spain following the financial crisis reveals a substantial increase in these rates that outstrip the underlying historic trends (Lopez Bernal et al, 2013). Moreover, Lopez Bernal et al (2013) speculate that these rates may further rise as data post-2010 are released that cover the time period where the greatest cuts to public spending have occurred. A key mechanism for the increase in suicide during times of crisis would appear to be closely related to an increase in unemployment (Stuckler et al, 2009). We may understand this relationship as a result of the sudden deterioration in social status and the difficulties in adjusting to the gap between societal expectations and an individual's ability to realise them, particularly when a society fails to help those individuals to readjust to the loss of a job and income (Eckersley and Dear, 2002).

Again there is a notable variance between the regimes in terms of the prevalence of suicide. An ANOVA of suicide (log scale) on regime demonstrated evidence of a difference between regimes unlikely to be due to chance ($p<0.0002$). The rate of suicide in the meso-corporatist regime (see Table 4.2) is significantly higher than all others (and the rate in post-socialist regime higher than in neoliberal and southern

Table 4.2: Suicide by regime

Regime	Suicide		Number obs
	Mean (SD)	Median (range)	
1 Neoliberal	9.15 (5.87)	9.15 (5–13.3)	2
2 Liberal	10.63 (2.04)	11.05 (6.7–12.4)	6
3 Post-socialist corporatist	16.62 (4.48)	16.05 (10.8–23.3)	6
4 Southern corporatist	6.18 (2.50)	6.10 (3.2–9.3)	4
5 Meso-corporatist	27.30 (8.79)	27.30 (21.1–33.5)	2
6 Northern corporatist	13.56 (3.57)	13.90 (9.2–17.7)	5
7 Social democratic	12.95 (2.91)	11.65 (11.2–17.3)	4

corporatist regimes), and the rate within the southern corporatist regime lower than the post-socialist, meso-corporatist, northern corporatist and social democratic regimes.

While the southern corporatist regime appears to outperform other regimes, some caution needs to be adopted in relation to these figures. As Eckersley and Dear (2002) note, suicide may be under-reported or recorded in Catholic countries such as Italy and Spain because of the Church's teachings on and attitude towards suicide. Moreover, the proscription of suicide may affect greater levels of social regulation that serve to inhibit fatal forms of self-harm. The data presented in this section draw on data for 2010 or the nearest available year; however, this analysis does not capture the subsequent rises experienced in the suicide rates in individual nation states as a result of the credit crunch. Therefore, the impact of the crisis on nation states in the southern corporatist regime, among the hardest hit by the credit crunch and era of austerity, cannot be fully explored here – although, as noted above, the inability of these nation states to protect populations against the corrosive impacts of unemployment and loss of status have been exposed in recent analyses.

In contrast, the social democratic regime appears to perform less well than other regimes. However, these rates are somewhat distorted by the fact that Finland has a high suicide rate (17.3 per 100,000), with relatively lower rates for Sweden (11.7), Denmark (11.2) and Norway (11.6). Helliwell (2007) observes that Scandinavian suicide rates have been traditionally skewed by high Finnish suicide rates, which masks the historical improvements made in Swedish and Danish rates that fell between 1980 and 2000, falling by one-third in Sweden and by one-half in Denmark during this period. In terms of Finland's persistently high rates of suicide, numerous authors have pointed to the high levels of firearm ownership – the availability of a lethal means to take one's life – as an explanatory factor (Johnson et al, 2000). Having said this, it is interesting that Stuckler et al's analysis of time series data (2009) revealed that the response of suicide rates to changes in unemployment varied greatly between nation states, yet Finland and Sweden appeared to best protect their populations against the impacts of unemployment on suicide rates. Stuckler et al conclude that, 'the commitments of the governments of Sweden and Finland to social support during times of crises ... could have a role' in reducing suicide rates, in particular expenditure on social protection and active labour market programmes (2009, p 321).

It is interesting that the neoliberal and liberal regimes, that are the most unequal and the least cohesive (given the Durkheimian legacy), appear to have relatively low overall rates of suicide. It is perhaps the case that the transition to more individualised social forms that many of these societies have undertaken in recent history provided spikes in rates of suicide. As Eckersley and Dear (2002, p 1900) argue, the shift towards individualism that occurred in many liberal societies were, arguably, responsible for the persistently high rates of suicides among young men experienced by some nation states:

> ... the rapid rise in male youth suicide in countries such as Australia, New Zealand and the UK (but not, interestingly, the US) in the 1980s, when (individualistic) neo-liberal, market-dominated doctrines became politically dominant. The steep rise in male youth suicide during this period is especially marked in New Zealand ... the country which adopted the most radical and rapid economic reforms.

Societies that reify individualism create unrealistic and unattainable images of unrestrained individuals exercising their boundless freedom and choices. Yet, as Eckersley and Dear (2002, pp 1901-2) note, 'the openness and diversity of modern life can mean adolescents today are confronted with an overload of developmental tasks', whereby excessive freedom can result in dissatisfaction. Such dissatisfaction is compounded by the realisation that, for many, these choices are essentially illusory, without the capacity or resources to act on them. However, the fact remains that aggregate suicide rates for both regimes remain relatively low, particularly in contrast to the rates of intentional violence observed in the previous section for these regimes. Wilkinson and Pickett (2010, p 175) observe that 'suicide is often inversely related to homicide', which would certainly appear to be borne out by the high homicide rates of the neoliberal regime provided earlier in this chapter, and comparatively low rates of suicide. Moreover, the US has one of the highest rates of homicide and an unremarkable rate of suicide. Wilkinson and Pickett (2010, p 175) surmise that '... there seems to be something to the psychological cliché that anger sometimes goes in and sometimes goes out: do you blame yourself or others for things that go wrong?' – arguably, these processes of internalisation/ externalisation will depend on a host of cultural variables.

This notion seems to gain greater credence due to the fact that both Japan and Korea, conversely, have low homicide rates and the highest rates of suicide. Suicide rates in the meso-corporatist regime must be understood as a product of the particular collectivist form that these societies take. The group is far more important than the individual. Confucianism is still heavily influential – dictating the basic unit of society is not the individual, but in Japanese it literally means 'house', where individuals are subsumed into larger social units, the family, the school, the company and so on (Amagasa et al, 2005). It is therefore far more important to forge one's identity through a group rather than as an autonomous individual being. Given the importance of the group, an individual's self-worth is judged through their contribution to the group. Shame then plays a fundamental role within these societies, particularly when someone is unable to contribute towards the activities of the group in the ways that would be expected – loss of face in relation to family members or colleagues is to be avoided at all costs. It is also an important contextual factor within the rates of suicide – particularly in relation to work. For instance, the Japanese work model is based around 'lifetime employment, a pay scale based on seniority, and loyalty to the employer. As a result, employees do not usually change companies' (Amagasa et al, 2005, p 163). Thus, membership to such organisations defines identity, but also demands loyalty, which means that individuals are forced to assess themselves in this respect. Thus, Amagasa et al (2005, p 162) observe that, 'the collapse of the Japanese economy in the early 1990s, restructuring and downsizing of companies ... placed workers under enormous pressures', which gave rise to *karojisatsu* (work-related suicide) as a consequence of overwork and the pressures that this created in individuals' personal lives. Indeed, the East Asian financial crisis of the late 1990s is estimated to have resulted in 10,000 excess suicides in Japan, Hong Kong and Korea (Chang et al, 2009). These increases in suicide were closely associated with rises in unemployment rates as a consequence of the crisis, and had a disproportionate impact on men, with male suicide rates in Korea more than doubling, from 19 per 100,000 in 1995 to 50 in 2010 (OECD, 2011).

Whereas homicide was presented above as a violent act synonymous with fragmented and individualised societies, it would appear that high suicide rates are the product of specific collectivist forms that reify the individual contributions and demonstrations of loyalty to the social group, creating often unbearable pressures to conform to these expectations. Some exceptions have been noted here, particularly the role of individualism in youth suicides, as well as the role of social protection in enabling some societies to lessen the impact of crises and peaks in unemployment rates on suicide rates.

Infant mortality

As with the previous physical harms, rates of infant mortality are viewed as important markers of social development, and are reflective of broader forms of social organisation. Infant mortality could easily be conceived as the tragic outcomes of individual biology and therefore a result of the 'lottery of life'. However, there is an explicit acknowledgement within the epidemiological literature that while individual level factors are important, such as maternal age and smoking, as well as biological markers, in particular, low birth weight, broader social determinants appear to have a significant impact on these rates. As Conley and Springer suggest, 'sociodemographic factors are generally believed to have an indirect affect on IM [infant mortality] mediated through individual-level variables located primarily in the biological domain' (2001, p 772). It is true to say that infant mortality rates have declined drastically in advanced nation states since the 1960s, with improvements attributed to rising standards of living, medical and technological advances (Arntzen and Andersen, 2004). However, these advancements have been uneven, and infant mortality rates remain patterned, with clear disparities in rates between nation states, which leads Coburn to conclude that '... there is a telling loss of life between the best and worst case scenarios' (2004, p 50). Given these disparities and the clear evidence presented of the social determinants that influence these rates, it would appear to be a sound assumption that many of these deaths are preventable events.

The reported variation in infant mortality rates appears to be sustained by the regime types presented. An ANOVA of the rate of infant deaths (log scale) on regime demonstrated strong evidence of a difference between regimes unlikely to be due to chance ($p<0.0001$). The average rate within the neoliberal regime was significantly higher than that of all other regimes, with the social democratic regime type demonstrating the lowest levels. This appears to confirm existing work that has applied welfare regime types to infant mortality rates, which equally demonstrates that social democratic countries appear to achieve lower rates than other regime types (Conley and Springer, 2001) (see Table 4.3).

Again, it is important to identify the features of these societies that appear to reduce these rates. Beginning with social solidarity, inequality ($p<0.000$) demonstrated a significant association with infant mortality rates (log scale). Thus, the more unequal a society, the higher the rates of infant mortality they are likely to demonstrate. This finding is supported by previous studies, as Arntzen and Andersen report, '... the systematic tendency is that the higher people are located in the social hierarchy, whether measured by social group, educational level, or income, the lower the infant mortality rate' (2004, p 385). Arntzen and Andersen proceed to explain that our resources and material living conditions have a significant impact on our opportunity to lead healthy lifestyles: '... the mechanisms may be behaviour/lifestyle factors, such as smoking, drinking, dietary habits, and physical exercise, which clearly are associated with adverse reproductive outcomes' (2004, p 387).

To further develop the observation made earlier in relation to the variance of rates between regimes, Figure 4.5 demonstrates interesting regime clusters – while the social democratic regime member countries cluster around low levels of inequality/infant mortality, southern, northern, meso and post-socialist corporatist countries appear densely packed around this point. Two distinct clusters emerge as the line of best-fit gradient increases: first, the liberal regime and then, the neoliberal regime.

Within the epidemiological literature, some contestation exists around the importance of inequality for understanding the variance in infant mortality deaths. Rather, these rates are more likely to be

Table 4.3: Infant mortality rates by regime

Regime	Infant deaths/1,000 live births	
	Mean (SD)	Median (range)
1 Neoliberal	10.70 (3.14)	10.10 (7.90–14.10)
2 Liberal	4.88 (0.98)	4.85 (3.80–6.60)
3 Post-socialist corporatist	4.08 (1.40)	4.15 (2.50–5.70)
4 Southern corporatist	3.43 (0.25)	3.30 (3.30–3.80)
5 Meso-corporatist	3.05 (0.64)	3.05 (2.60–3.50)
6 Northern corporatist	3.60 (0.20)	3.70 (3.30–3.80)
7 Social democratic	2.95 (0.70)	2.65 (2.50–4.00)

Figure 4.5: Infant mortality/inequality

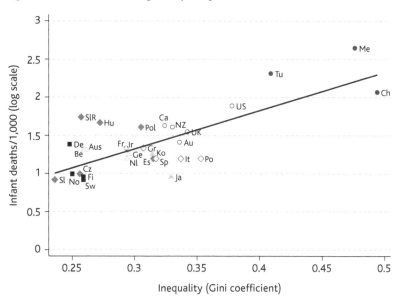

determined by other factors, for example, welfare or health policies that have a direct impact on population health status (Conley and Springer, 2001; Chung and Muntaner, 2006). Figure 4.6 demonstrates that higher levels of social expenditure would appear to be associated with low rates of infant mortality (log scale) ($p<0.0001$).

It may well be that social expenditure serves to mitigate the aspects of inequality that determine poor health outcomes. Social spending that serves to decommodify aspects of our lives enables healthy lifestyles to be pursued, but also promotes social capital that is likely to facilitate successful interpretation of health promotion initiatives. Unsurprisingly, increased healthcare expenditure also demonstrates an association with decreasing levels of infant mortality (log scale) ($p=0.013$), although it should be noted that this is not as statistically significant as social expenditure. This finding resonates with previous studies; in particular, Conley and Springer's cross-sectional analysis of 30 years of healthcare expenditure data demonstrates '... each additional 1% in per capita health care spending – in the base models – is associated with a reduction in the LBW [low birth weight] rate by 0.129% and the IMR [infant mortality rate] by 0.184%' (2001, p 788).

This said, as Figure 4.7 reveals, clusters that appear to suggest the relationship between health expenditure and infant mortality rates might be more complex. For example, the US, New Zealand and Canada exhibit high levels of health expenditure, yet high rates of

Figure 4.6: Infant mortality/social expenditure

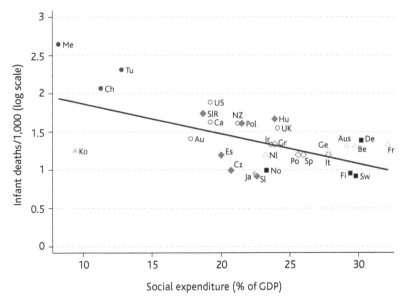

Figure 4.7: Infant mortality/health expenditure

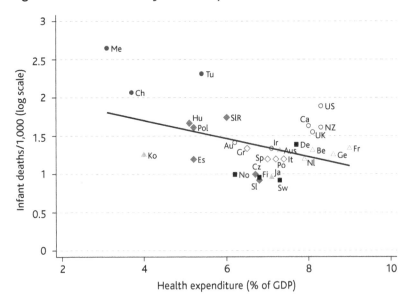

mortality. This may be explained by the administrative costs associated with insurance-based health schemes, and the relative proportions of health budgets in these countries spent on the expense of determining eligibility for health services. Conversely, social democratic countries such as Sweden, Finland and Norway demonstrate moderate levels of health expenditure, yet some of the lowest infant mortality rates. Again, we may speculate about the impact of broader patterns of social expenditure, and in particular, the high levels of expenditure on social services that are likely to promote post-natal health through alternative policy mechanisms.

Obesity

Over the past 20 years, rates of obesity across advanced industrial societies have universally increased, and many health commentators refer to obesity as a 'global epidemic', with emerging economies and many developing nations demonstrating increasing levels of obesity. In recent years, rates of obesity have rapidly increased, and in the space of a few years, many countries have demonstrated a doubling in their prevalence rates, with over a quarter of the adult population in the developed world with a BMI (body mass index) score of 30 and above (Pickett et al, 2005). Underlying the growth in obesity are two related processes: increased consumption of highly refined foods that are high in protein and saturated fats and low in complex carbohydrates; combined with significant reductions in energy expenditure associated with the increasingly sedentary nature of contemporary lifestyles characterised by high levels of motorised transport, less physical forms of work and leisure time dominated by inactive hobbies.

Obesity has a significant impact on the experience of secondary physical harms, increasing the risk of type II diabetes, cardiovascular disease, hypertension, gallbladder disease and some cancers (Pickett et al, 2005). As Wang et al report, every 'additional $5kg/m^2$ in BMI increases a man's risk of oesophageal cancer by 52% and for colon cancer by 24%, and in women, endometrial cancer by 59%, gall bladder cancer by 59%, and postmenopausal breast cancer by 12%' (2011, p 815). In terms of life expectancy, it is estimated that an obese person's life span is 2-4 years shorter than someone with a weight within the normal range, whereas someone who is severely obese is likely to lose 8-10 years. Perhaps as significant is the impact of obesity on life-limiting illnesses – in a study of 10 European countries, the chance of disability for those who are obese was estimated to be nearly twice that of those with normal weight. Wang et al's analyses (2011) suggest that a hypothetical 1 per cent reduction in weight across the population that would equate to an approximate loss of 1kg for an adult of average weight would have profound effects. For example, 'a 1% BMI reduction across the US population would avoid up to 2.1-

2.4 million incident cases of diabetes, 1.4-1.7 million cardiovascular diseases, and 73,000-127,000 cases of cancer, with a gain of about 16 million QALYs [quality-adjusted life years]' (Wang et al, 2011, p 820).

Obesity not only inflicts considerable physical harms; it places a significant and increasing burden on healthcare systems. The rising prevalence of obesity in advanced industrialised countries carries considerable healthcare costs and implications for future healthcare provision. Wang et al estimate that obesity-related disorders in the US will cost US$28 billion annually by 2020, rising to US$60 billion per year by 2030 (2011, p 821). Similarly in the UK, the costs of treating obesity-related disorders will add £648 million annually to existing figures by 2020, and an estimated £2 billion by 2030. Alongside these costs can be added the loss of productivity due to obesity-related disorders. As suggested above, this comes at a cost for individuals through the life-limiting illnesses that serve to compromise the realisation of human potential, laying waste to the most productive years of people's lives. Wang et al, drawing on existing survey data, estimate a loss of 1.7-3 million productive person years in US adults of working age, which equates to an economic cost of US$390-580 billion (2011, p 821).

A great deal has been written that seeks to explain the rising prevalence of obesity. As a number of commentators have noted, the rapidity of this increase is indicative of environmental and societal factors, rather than genetic changes within the population – although genetic factors may influence an individual's predisposition to weight gain (Pickett et al, 2005). Thus, a consensus emerges from the extensive literature on obesity that identifies the ways in which 'obesogenic environment(s)' have taken an almost universal hold within capitalist societies. This environment has led to increased calorific intakes and declining rates of energy expenditure – yet important structural transformations within our societies underlie this calorific surplus. A variety of organisational features of societies will be discussed in relation to contrasting rates of obesity below; however, the global nature of this pandemic points us towards an obvious starting point being the corollary development of global multinational food companies and markets. As Friel (2007, p 1241) notes:

> The liberalised trade opened many more countries to the international market. Food subsidies here arguably distorted the food supply in favour of less healthy foodstuffs such as those with high in saturated fats and transnational food

companies have flooded the global market with cheap to
produce, energy dense, nutrient empty food....

Hawkes (2006) has extended this analysis largely in relation to low
and middle-income countries; nevertheless, many of the overarching
analytical points are relevant here. Hawkes identifies three features of
globalisation that have contributed to the development of 'obesogenic
environment(s)'. First, the 'production and exchange of goods',
rather than being subdivided among a range of companies, are
now conglomerated into single forms, in the guise of transnational
corporations (TNCs), concentrating immense power into the hands of
a few, distorting competition within markets and altering the regulatory
relationship between nations states and markets (Hawkes, 2006, p 7).
Second, 'the flow of investment across borders' in the form of FDI
(foreign direct investment) has dramatically increased since the 1980s,
and this investment has mainly been focused on food processing, in
turn lowering the costs of these foods and funding marketing strategies
– thus, making processed foods available to more people (Hawkes,
2006, p 7). Third, 'the global communication of information' in
relation to energy-dense foods has served to shape consumption
patterns – evidenced by the rise in global advertising budgets from
1980 to 2004, where expenditure grew from US$216 billion to
US$512 billion (Hawkes, 2006, p 13).

   However, the pressures created by global capital and the global chains
of food production have not been uniformly felt. Between nation states
there is considerable disparity in the rates of obesity, to the extent that
Korea has the lowest self-reported rate of 2 per 100,000 population,
whereas the US has the highest rate, at 28 per 100,000. Comparing
regime types in relation to obesity is somewhat fraught due to missing
cases in the neoliberal and meso-corporatist regimes. Nevertheless, an
ANOVA of obesity on regime demonstrated evidence of a difference
between regimes unlikely to be due to chance (p=0.001). Obesity was
significantly higher within the liberal regime than all other regimes.
In particular, it is clear that northern corporatist and social democratic
regimes exhibit considerably lower levels of obesity than the liberal
regime (see Table 4.4).

   Countries that have lower levels of obesity are able to better address
through policy and the preservation of local culture the energy surplus
created by processes of industrialisation and globalisation discussed
above. Korea exhibits low levels of obesity, which is commonly
believed to be, in part, explained by the customary diet that is low in
saturated fats (Kim et al, 2005), although it should be noted that this

Table 4.4: Obesity by regime

Regime	Obesity Mean (SD)	Number obs
1 Neoliberal	12.00	1
2 Liberal	20.45 (5.66)	4
3 Post-socialist corporatist	17.00 (1.79)	6
4 Southern corporatist	14.50 (3.11)	4
5 Meso-corporatist	2.00	1
6 Northern corporatist	13.00 (1.58)	5
7 Social democratic	13.00 (2.45)	4

picture is changing, as over the last 30 years principle dietary foods – rice, vegetables and fish – are being replaced with processed foods heavy in saturated fats (Kim, et al, 2005).

Nation states in the northern corporatist and social democratic regimes that exhibit lower levels of obesity are notable for policies in relation to the regulation of the food industry or that encourage non-sedentary forms of transport. Norway exhibits the lowest rate of obesity behind Korea. Norway established a proactive policy approach that successfully reversed consumption patterns based on high-fat, energy-dense diets through a combination of healthy food subsidies, price manipulation, retail regulations, nutrition labelling, and public health education (Friel et al, 2007). Similarly, countries that have invested heavily in non-sedentary forms of transport equally appear to have protected their populations from higher rates of obesity. There are therefore significant differences between the countries in terms of their transport policy, and in particular, provision for active modes, such as cycling. As the existing literature demonstrates, policies that make cycling safe and convenient are more likely to encourage participation, such as policies that have ensured provision in Dutch, Danish and German cities of 'separate cycling facilities along heavily travelled roads and at intersections, combined with extensive traffic calming of residential neighbourhoods' (Pucher and Buehler, 2008, p 523). As Pucher and Buehler's analysis demonstrates, this has profound impacts, so that 'Americans and Britons cycle for only 2% of their trips shorter than 2.5 km, compared to 37% in the Netherlands, 27% in Denmark and 14% in Germany ... that pattern also holds for the progressively longer trip distance categories' (2008, p 498).

In contrast, the liberal regime, as noted above, demonstrates markedly higher levels of obesity than other regime types, in particular, the member nation states US, Australia and Canada. In some respects this is not surprising for two principal reasons. First, a growing body of evidence relates obesity to inequality. Thus, as Friel et al note, 'a person or group's place in the social hierarchy influences behavioural choices which are governed by the material and psychosocial choices provided by the complex system of the food, built and social environments' (2007, p 1242). Therefore, the psychosocial impacts of inequality often serve to influence the prevalence of obesity due to: increased risk of central obesity resulting from particular low-cost/high-energy foods; fewer opportunities for physical exercise; the inability to access foodstuffs necessary for a healthy lifestyle; and the physiological effects of stress (Pickett et al, 2005). It follows that those countries that have higher levels of inequality raise the vulnerability of their population to the experience of obesity, a point illustrated by Pickett et al's analysis of 11 advanced capitalist societies, which observes the 'USA had the steepest social gradient in obesity and greatest income inequality, and Sweden the smallest of each' (2005, p 673). Second, liberal nation states tend towards lighter forms of market regulation, and are therefore more likely to be prone to the potentially damaging consequences of the globalisation of food production discussed above. Indeed, the extent to which nation states are willing to regulate the consumption of processed foods appears to be instrumental in controlling rates of obesity. Rosenheck's systematic review provides compelling evidence of the 'independent role of fast food consumption contributing to increased caloric intake, hastening rates of weight gain or obesity' (2008, p 546). Yet in the US in particular there has been an unfettered proliferation of fast food outlets:

> Fast food outlets have increased from about 30,000 in 1970 to more than 233,000 locations in the USA in 2004 and have been classified as the most rapidly expanding sector of the US food distribution centre. Correspondingly, money spent on out-of-home food expenditures represented 25% of total food spending in 1970 and subsequently increased to 47.5% of total food spending in 1999. (Rosenheck, 2008, p 535)

It would appear that the liberal regime is less likely to provide environments where healthy foodstuffs are readily and widely available, or the sort of living environments whereby healthy and active lifestyles are achievable. Those countries that are organised in these ways would appear to have achieved lower rates of obesity.

Road traffic injuries

Road traffic injuries account for an estimated 1.3 million deaths annually, which represents a rate of nearly 20 per 100,000 of the population (Chandran et al, 2010). These deaths form the largest proportion of unintentional injury deaths, according to the WHO classification, contributing a third of these deaths globally (Chandran et al, 2010). In addition, road traffic injuries constitute 41 per cent of the total child injury deaths in rich nations (Christie et al, 2007). Projections from WHO suggest that while road traffic injuries were the ninth leading cause of death, accounting for 2.2 per cent of global deaths in 2004, they are likely to rise to the fifth leading cause by 2030, resulting in 3.6 per cent of global deaths (Chandran et al, 2010, p 112). The predicted rise in global deaths is mainly due to the rapid urbanisation and motorisation taking place in many lower and middle-income countries, while in many advanced industrial societies, death rates from road traffic injuries appear to be falling (Ameratunga et al, 2006). However, the downward trend in fatalities in many OECD countries has been accompanied by a rise in serious non-fatal injuries. Ameratunga et al's analysis of Norwegian road traffic injury rates for the period 1992-97 reveals a decrease in death rates, while the rate of permanent impairment/disability from accidents rose dramatically as a consequence of improvements made to the safety of vehicle design, such as the introduction of air bags, and the quality and availability of first aid and acute emergency care (Ameratunga et al, 2006).

It is worth noting that the improvements in safety in OECD countries are not equally distributed, and the harms of motorised transport are often unevenly distributed across populations. Ameratunga et al note that in many countries, 'steep class gradients by socioeconomic status are noted for morbidity and fatality from road traffic injury with rates being higher in lower social classes' (2006, p 1535). In many respects, income determines vulnerability as a road user. Thus, as UNICEF (2001, p 16) note in relation to children:

> On the roads, poor children are more likely to live in built up areas with greater traffic densities, and more likely to travel on foot or by bike. For child car occupants, the economic differential intervenes in the form of newer, larger, heavier cars and the greater likelihood of modern, properly installed child restraints, passenger air bags, crumple zones, and side-impact protection bars.

However, an irony of the growth of sports utility vehicles (SUVs) is that while they purport to offer greater levels of safety to its occupants, the consequences for those involved in collisions with SUVs, particularly pedestrians, are increased risks of serious and fatal injury due to the weight and design of these vehicles (Ballesteros et al, 2004).

Given the scale of injuries outlined, it is unsurprising that the implications of road traffic injuries for healthcare systems are considerable. Analyses provided by the Transport Research Laboratory revealed that the average annual costs of road traffic injuries are approximately 2 per cent of gross national product (GNP) in heavily motorised societies (Jacobs et al, 2000). The annual global economic cost of road traffic injuries is estimated to be over US$518 billion (Ameratunga et al, 2006). The costs of road traffic injuries are also reflected in the loss of productive years of human activity; due to the fact that 15- to 44-year-olds account for over half of road traffic fatalities, these injuries contribute to almost 70 per cent of potential years of life lost in many countries (Ameratunga et al, 2006). Moreover, globally 59 per cent of disability-adjusted life years lost resulted from road traffic injuries (Ameratunga et al, 2006).

An ANOVA of road traffic fatalities (log scale) on regime demonstrated no evidence of any differences between regimes ($p=0.53$) (see Table 4.5). Indeed, within regime type great disparities were noted in death rates per 100,000 of the population. While regimes did not demonstrate significant associations with road traffic fatality rates, important variance existed between nation states. Indeed, the worst performing nation states, the Russian Federation (24.7 per 100,000), Mexico (17) and the US (14.6), have fatality rates 6, 4 and 3.5 times greater than the least harmful, the Netherlands (4), UK (4) and Sweden (4.1). Even when exposure to risk is taken into account, the differences between nation states remain. For example, in the US,

Table 4.5: Road traffic deaths by regime

Regime	Road traffic deaths		Number obs
	Mean (SD)	Median (range)	
1 Neoliberal	9.35 (6.46)	7.25 (4.3–18.6)	4
2 Liberal	8.45 (3.94)	7.95 (4.0–14.6)	6
3 Post-socialist corporatist	7.38 (1.52)	7.10 (5.8–10.2)	6
4 Southern corporatist	9.00 (1.81)	9.10 (6.7–11.1)	4
5 Meso-corporatist	8.90 (6.79)	8.90 (4.1–13.7)	2
6 Northern corporatist	6.64 (2.52)	6.80 (4–10.6)	5
7 Social democratic	5.00 (0.75)	5.00 (4.1–5.9)	4

where children undertake relatively little travel as pedestrians, injury rates remain high, in stark contrast to Norway, where children walk long distances, while maintaining low levels of injury (Christie et al, 2007). Similarly, in the Netherlands, with high levels of child cyclists, they have relatively low levels of fatality, again in contrast to the US, with low levels of child cyclists and relatively high rates of injury (Christie et al, 2007).

This variance suggests that to some extent road traffic injuries can be 'designed out' of our societies through a combination of 'engineering, legislation, enforcement and education' (Langley, 2001, p 269). However, in many nation states, the levels of fatalities that persist can be explained as a result of the primacy afforded to motorised transport:

> In many countries, the planning of road transport systems and urban development has not accommodated the needs of all road users. Frequently motorized transport has been catered for when developing transport infrastructure, while non-motorized transport and other uses of transport and land space ... little consideration for the needs of the communities they pass through – such as where high-speed roads have been built passing close to schools or residential areas. (Toroyan and Peden, 2007, p 9)

Thus, nation states that have lowered speed limits in residential areas have effectively reduced road traffic injuries. For example, when the UK introduced 20mph (32kmh) speed limits, this led to a 70 per cent reduction in child pedestrian accidents and a 50 per cent decrease in accidents involving child cyclists (UNICEF, 2001). Quite simply, the higher the speed a vehicle is travelling, the less time drivers have to react, and the greater the injury inflicted on the individuals involved in the collision. Speed can also be minimised through infrastructural interventions, such as speed humps, mini roundabouts and pedestrian crossings (Toroyan and Peden, 2007). Thus, cycling fatalities in the Netherlands have been minimised through the implementation of road architecture that has lowered urban speed limits and separated cyclists from fast-moving vehicular traffic (Pucher and Buehler, 2008). Finally, the enforcement of safety legislation in relation to speed, drink-driving, safety helmet use, seat belts and child restraints are also likely to determine road traffic injury rates. For example, in a recent survey of enforcement of road safety legislation, 28 countries have coverage of the five areas listed above, yet only four countries

(Estonia, Finland, France and Portugal) reported enforcing these laws in an effective manner (WHO, 2013).

Personal motorised transport may be viewed as an expression of freedom and autonomy in any capitalist society; however, it comes at a high price, particularly when societies evolve to promote this form of transport as the principal mode. It would appear that societies are able to reduce the levels of harm successfully by promoting alternative modes of transport and organising spaces that are not dominated by fast-moving traffic.

Conclusion

Importantly for the central arguments of the book in relation to the preventable nature of harm, there appear to be considerable disparities between nation states in respect of particular harms. It is certainly not always the case that these disparities are consistently pronounced between nation states, particularly in relation to homicide rates, whereby, albeit for some notable examples, these rates remain consistent among the nation states included in the study. It is important not to overstate difference, particularly as many nation states appear to converge around the mean; nevertheless, divergence does exist, and the analysis presented here has sought to identify why this may be the case.

The data presents a complex picture, with nation states at times demonstrating contrasting and contradictory levels of performance in relation to specific physical harms. Nevertheless, a pattern begins to emerge in relation to the regimes and physical harms analysed here. The neoliberal regime, and to a lesser extent, the liberal regime, demonstrate consistently higher levels of physical harms – with the exception of suicides – whereas northern corporatist and social democratic regimes have consistently lower levels of physical harm. With the remaining corporatist regimes it is more difficult to discern such clear aggregate patterns of harm production.

There are some tentative conclusions that can be drawn here (developed in greater detail in Chapter Six), that serve to explain the reasons that particular societies appear to produce greater levels of physical harm, where others are able to minimise this harm. First, societies that demonstrate high levels of *decommodification*, in the Esping Andersen sense of the term (in other words, welfare spend that means that individuals are not reliant on the market as the only means of needs satisfaction), seem better equipped to protect their populations. For example, the impact of social spending is evidenced in relation to physical harms of homicide and infant mortality rates. Second, *chaotic societies*, those societies that eschew social organisation in exchange for individual freedoms, appear to be more harmful. Thus, those societies that choose to plan urban development and transport to accommodate all road users have lower rates of road traffic deaths. Similarly, those societies that regulate food distribution have lower rates of obesity. Third, *fragmented societies*, those societies that demonstrate low levels of trust and high levels of inequality, appear to generate greater levels of harm – particularly in relation to homicide and infant mortality rates.

Finally, the physical harms reviewed in this chapter are subject to some notable fluctuations across time. While homicide and suicide rates remain relatively stable, and obesity has risen, aggregate levels of road traffic deaths and infant mortality rates have fallen. The falls experienced in the latter harms arguably result from the development of technologies within car safety and medical care, and may demonstrate support for an argument that capitalism generates investment and innovation that serves to protect and reduce aggregate harms. To some extent this is true; however, markets only offer safe technologies for those who can afford them – indeed, an irony of the safety offered to the drivers and passengers of SUVs are the increased numbers of pedestrian deaths that result as a consequence of collisions with these vehicles. Similarly, the advent of medical technology and practices that increase the likelihood of infant survival rates require a healthcare system that provides an equality of access to these technologies – otherwise, the harm reduction impacts are muted.

FIVE

Harm reduction regimes and the production of autonomy and relational harms

Autonomy and relational harms are less obviously injurious than physical harms, whereby a death or loss of physical functioning is prima facie harmful. Thus, this chapter in part serves to explain why the particular harms that are presented here should be considered to be injurious. Autonomy harms, as explained in detail in Chapter Two, result from situations that fundamentally disrupt our attempts to achieve self-actualisation. It is argued that self-actualisation is made possible through the achievement of a sufficient level of autonomy, which ensures an individual has the ability to formulate choices and the capacity to act on these. The chapter identifies relative poverty, child poverty, financial insecurity, youth unemployment and long working hours as conditions in which our autonomy is compromised due to lack of resources or opportunities. Relational harms, as described in Chapter Two, result from either an enforced exclusion from social networks, or the injurious nature of misrecognition. Given the paucity of comparative data – discussed in Chapter Three – social isolation is the only relational harm considered here. Thus, the analysis provided relates to the injuries that result when we are unable to sustain relationships or some form of meaningful human contact.

The chapter contributes to the empirical interrogation of the notion of preventable harm; again, as with the previous chapter, this analysis focuses on the variance between regimes and nation states in terms of the extent of these harms. It is certainly the case, particularly in relation to autonomy harms, that these are inextricably intertwined with the extraction of surplus value – a process integral to the capitalist economic model. Yet there is considerable variance in the experience of these harms, and, therefore, the analytical focus of the chapter falls on the ways in which different societies organise the features of the mode of production, to alter the forms that surplus value takes, as well as the extent to which our reliance on markets for income and services is tempered by welfare systems.

Relative poverty

Poverty is probably 'the largest source of social harm; it causes more deaths, diseases, suffering and misery than any other social phenomena' (Gordon, 2004, p 251). While the most injurious form is undoubtedly the absolute deprivation most commonly experienced in lower-income countries, poverty in its relative form causes untold damage to the lives of those affected in advanced industrialised societies. Relative poverty results when individuals command an insufficient level of income that 'cannot obtain, at all or sufficiently, the condition of life, that is, the diets, amenities, standards and services – which allow them to play the roles, participate in the relationships and follow the customary behaviour which is expected of them by virtue of their membership of society' (Townsend, 1993, p 36). Thus, the notion of relative poverty describes an enforced exclusion from the activities and standards taken for granted as norms by mainstream society, which moves our understanding of poverty beyond a notion of mere subsistence. As Veit-Wilson notes, 'material resources may support the physical organism but it is the full range of social and psychological resources which are required for the experience of humanity' (1999, p 85). Without doubt, relative poverty should be considered an autonomy harm; it is not difficult to imagine how this state has an impact on an individual's ability to achieve the desired forms of self-actualisation, through the constraints placed on life choices, through the absence of the necessary resources to act on these choices. Evidence also suggests that relative poverty has a negative impact on individuals' development, explored in greater detail in relation to child poverty, in terms of our education (Sutton et al, 2007; Muschamp et al, 2009; Wikeley et al, 2009) and the acquisition of skills and qualifications across the life course (Page, 2000; Saunders et al, 2006).

The secondary harms resulting from relative poverty are well documented. There is an extensive literature that details the impacts of financial hardship on physical health; as Marmot (2005) notes, this creates dramatic differences in life expectancy within populations due to the availability of healthy lifestyles and the impact of poor housing conditions and environments on our life chances. In the US the gap in life expectancy between the richest and poorest sections of society is 20 years (Marmot, 2005, p 1099). Similarly in the UK, as Thomas et al's analysis discovered, 'by the year 2007 for every 100 people under the age of 65 dying in the best-off areas, 199 were dying in the poorest tenth of areas' (2010, p 3637). Moreover, the impact of poverty on mental health is also well documented, for example, studies have reported increased levels of depression, anxiety and phobias for those experiencing persistent hardship that result from the stress and anxieties caused by life on a low income, as well as the perception of personal failure and erosion of self-esteem (Baker and Taylor, 1997; Lynch et al, 1997; Payne, 2006). Beyond the health impacts reported here are the host of harmful social-psychological impacts of relative poverty, that result from ways in which the 'poor' are perceived, treated and portrayed by 'mainstream society'. The injurious nature of these social relations commonly result in feelings of shame (Fahmy and Pemberton, 2012), powerlessness (Cohen et al, 1992; Smith, 2005), and low self-esteem (Batty and Flint, 2010; Flint, 2010).

It may well be that relative poverty is an 'inevitable' consequence of capitalist organisation (Novak, 1988) – there are good reasons to have sympathies with this viewpoint, given that it stands to reason that the competition that capitalism engenders naturally results in 'winners and losers', and the 'losers' are as important to the whole system as the 'winners', given the vital function the reserve army of labour plays in suppressing wage levels and ultimately, in maintaining profit. Yet, as Lister (2003, p 23) argues, theoretically there is not necessarily a 'natural rate' of relative poverty, even within an unequal capitalist society:

> It is logically conceivable, though unlikely, that a society could be very unequal but without poverty, if all its members had the resources necessary to participate fully in society.

It is not the place to resolve this conundrum here, yet the point remains that while socioeconomic inequality cannot be designed out of capitalist society, there is nothing inevitable about relative poverty rates. In part, this can be evidenced by the dramatic differences in poverty rates from one society to another. An ANOVA of relative poverty on regime demonstrated strong evidence of a difference between regimes unlikely to be due to chance ($p<0.0001$). The percentage of households with income less than 60 per cent of the median income was notably higher within the neoliberal regime than the other regimes – with the exception of the meso-corporatist regime – and the post-socialist, northern corporatist and social democratic regimes are significantly lower than the others.

As in the previous chapter it is important to unpick the features of regimes that serve to determine the variety in rates between different formations. An obvious place to begin is the level of social expenditure

Table 5.1: Relative poverty by regime

Regime	Relative poverty, % of households with <60% median income Mean (SD)	Number obs
1 Neoliberal	25.33 (1.53)	3
2 Liberal	19.83 (2.64)	6
3 Post-socialist	14.33 (4.23)	6
4 Southern corporatist	19.25 (0.96)	4
5 Meso-corporatist	21.50 (0.71)	2
6 Northern corporatist	14.20 (1.30)	5
7 Social democratic	14.50 (1.73)	4

on benefits and services. There appears to be a strong association between social expenditure and relative poverty rates ($p<0.001$). Figure 5.1 demonstrates that those nation states that have higher levels of social expenditure exhibit lower rates of relative poverty. It is notable that social democratic and northern corporatist nation states cluster towards the high expenditure/low poverty point on the axis, while those regimes that have higher poverty rates, such as the neoliberal, liberal and meso–corporatist regimes, have lower levels of social expenditure. Accordingly, one would expect the southern corporatist regime to have lower poverty rates, given the rate of social expenditure. However, social expenditure may be reflective of high

Figure 5.1: Relative poverty/social expenditure

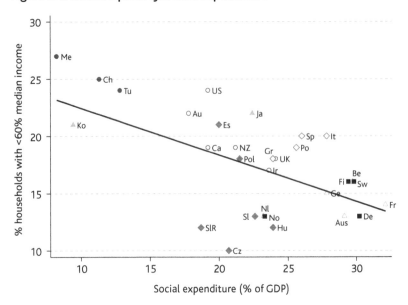

rates of unemployment experienced as a result of the credit crunch post-2008, rather than illustrative of the generosity of these systems.

As alluded to above, social spending as an aggregate only tells part of the story. Indeed, as noted, high levels of expenditure on the apparatus to deliver means-tested benefits and services does little to alleviate poverty. Rather, we need to unpick the extent of benefit generosity in different nation states. It is beyond the remit of the study to test a host of benefits here; however, when indicative measures for pensions and unemployment benefits generosity were deployed, these indicators did not demonstrate a relationship. Yet, more detailed studies exploring this relationship, for example, Scruggs and Allan, have found 'that more generous benefits for sickness and pensions are associated with large reductions in absolute poverty in advanced industrial societies' (2006, p 901). Similarly, Caminada et al's analysis stresses the importance of public income transfers, 'as an effective policy instrument in alleviating poverty' (2012, p 123).

While the primacy of social security systems in alleviating relative poverty cannot be doubted, there are further factors that should be considered. The relationship between trade union density and relative poverty demonstrates some evidence of an association ($p=0.042$). From Figure 5.2, it would appear that countries that have higher rates of trade union membership have lower rates of relative poverty. It is interesting that a group of northern corporatist countries, including Germany,

Figure 5.2: Relative poverty/trade union density

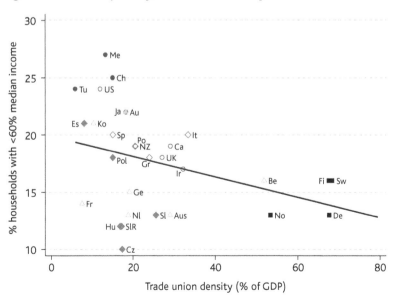

France, the Netherlands and Austria, appear to have low membership rates and low poverty rates. However, while union membership may be relatively low, using indicators of worker participation in workplace decision making and the power of trade unions over working conditions, this demonstrates that trade unions appear to have a strong influence over wages via workplace consultation and through collective bargaining agreements (Schroeder, 2009).

The near ubiquitous shift in unemployment policies towards 'welfare to work' or 'workfare' programmes privileges work as the principal policy mechanism to alleviate poverty and exclusion in many late capitalist societies. Therefore, wage levels are critical to safeguarding against relative poverty; moreover, trade unions would appear to play a vital role in protecting populations against 'in-work' poverty. This assertion is lent further credence when regression of 'in-work' poverty and trade union density are conducted, that exhibit a statistically significant association ($p=0.009$) – thus, increases in union membership appear to result in corresponding falls in 'in-work' poverty. Previous studies have also demonstrated such a relationship. Card et al's comparative study of wage inequality in three countries shows that the variations in male wage inequality between countries are related to trade union membership; they conclude that de-unionisation explains 'a significant part of the growth' in income inequality in the UK and US since the 1980s (2003, p 33).

Finally, it is interesting that those countries in which people demonstrate high levels of trust in others appear to have lower levels of poverty ($p=0.005$). It is not immediately obvious why this would necessarily be the case, and for some nation states, the association seems to be clearer than for others; for instance, social democratic countries exemplify this association, whereas post-socialist corporatist countries do not, such as the Czech Republic, Slovakia, Hungry and the Slovak Republic (see Figure 5.3). Nevertheless, an interpretation could be that high levels of trust underlie support for increased levels of social expenditure that serve to protect populations from high rates of relative poverty. Where trust in others is eroded, and there are relatively low levels of solidarity within society, then support for such expenditure is restricted; moreover, suspicion of others lends itself to heavily means-tested systems or targeted safety nets that provide often minimal forms of protection.

Figure 5.3: Relative poverty/trust

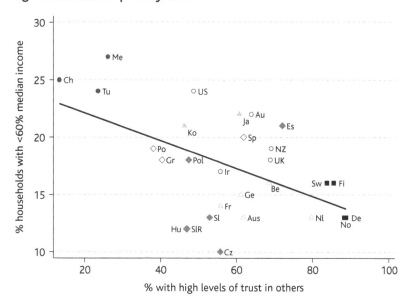

Child poverty

The meritocratic claims of capitalist societies give rise to the myths of social mobility that anyone, regardless of background, can transcend the initial position they are born into. The sad reality for many whose childhoods are blighted by poverty is that social mobility is more likely to be an illusion, rather than a reality. It follows, then, that child poverty, as for relative poverty, is a harmful condition for any child to exist within, seriously compromising the ability of children to develop in a range of positive ways. Just as with relative poverty, child poverty is inextricably linked with a host of harmful outcomes, as well as being inherently harmful in its own right. A substantial literature exists documenting the cumulative nature of harm across the life course that results from the experience of childhood deprivation. The causal path between child poverty and the experience of secondary harms is complex and contested. Nevertheless, as Bradshaw (2002) demonstrates, there is a significant difference in the experience of a range of harms and social problems between the 'poor' and 'non-poor':

> ... this is certainly the case for child mortality, low birth-weight, child accidental deaths, teenage pregnancy, housing conditions, educational attainment and youth suicide. It is probably the case for mental illness, though we do not have

good time series data on child mental health (or subjective feelings of well-being and self-esteem). (Bradshaw, 2002, p 137)

The point is that for many of the secondary harms that result from child poverty, it is very difficult to explore these interrelationships, as they manifest some way down the line at a later point in life. Nevertheless, a significant body of evidence points to the deleterious impact of child poverty on child development, and ultimately, on social mobility in later life. As Duncan et al demonstrate:

... income poverty has a strong association with a low level of preschool ability, which is associated with low test scores later in childhood as well as grade failure, school disengagement, and dropping out of school. (1998, p 420)

They proceed to explain that, '...preschool ability sets the stage for children's transition into the formal school system', so that children who do not possess a range of skills, such as counting, sorting, letters and so on, are immediately at a disadvantage which is difficult to overcome, as children tend to be classified into different ability groups from an early age (Duncan et al, 1998, p 420). From the outset, child poverty appears to structure our life opportunities and development, with the extent and severity of these deleterious impacts likely to be determined by the persistence and duration of episodes of childhood poverty (Bradley and Corwyn, 2002). Ultimately, these disadvantages play out in later life insofar as they pattern the experience of social mobility. Esping-Andersen and Wagner (2012) analysed the impacts of child poverty on mobility across different EU countries. While they observe little direct impact on adult income, child poverty did have a significant indirect effect as a result of children's eventual educational attainment – which confirms some of the findings detailed above. However, this indirect impact appears to be mitigated through more universal and generous welfare states – a reversal observed in social democratic countries (Jäntti et al, 2006; Esping-Andersen and Wagner, 2012) – while the relationship between child poverty and lower educational attainment persists in countries with comparatively less generous social security systems (in this study, specifically in relation to Italy, Spain and the UK; see Esping-Andersen and Wagner, 2012).

In many respects, the distribution of child poverty harms across regime type are similar, yet do not conform entirely to the patterns described in relation to relative poverty, as child-centred spending proves to be critical to this distribution, and this can differ from patterns of overall social expenditure.

An ANOVA of relative poverty on regime demonstrated strong evidence of a difference between regimes unlikely to be due to chance ($p<0.0001$). The percentage of households with children with an income less than 50 per cent of the median income was markedly higher within neoliberal regimes than all other regimes, and notably lower in the social democratic regime (see Table 5.2).

Beginning with child benefit expenditure, this appears to be associated with the experience of child poverty ($p=0.015$). As Figure 5.4 demonstrates, the greater the expenditure on child benefits, the lower the rate of child poverty. The US, Mexico and Poland have the highest rates of child poverty and exhibit some of the lowest child benefit expenditures. Yet the social democratic nation states that have the lowest rates of child poverty demonstrate moderate levels of child benefit. This can only really be explained in relation to the package of support that low-income families receive in these countries.

Moreover, as with all aggregate expenditure figures, these can hide important details, particularly in regard to the generosity of benefits or whether expenditure is dedicated to means testing. As Bradshaw suggests, those countries with the lowest child poverty rates have 'child benefit systems with certain common characteristics ... generous universal child benefits, in many cases with a large families gearing; comparatively generous out of work benefits or social assistance...' (2006, p 13). To some extent these details may be masked by the aggregate spending figures used here.

Similarly, child poverty rates appear to be significantly associated with child services expenditure ($p<0.001$). Thus, service expenditure would appear to protect households from the increased costs of raising children, offering important resources that supplement household

Table 5.2: Child poverty by regime

Regime	Child poverty, % of households with <50% median income Mean (SD)	Number obs
1 Neoliberal	23.50 (2.12)	2
2 Liberal	14.50 (3.94)	6
3 Post-socialist	13.00 (6.06)	4
4 Southern corporatist	15.75 (2.22)	4
5 Meso-corporatist	12.00 (2.83)	2
6 Northern corporatist	9.20 (1.30)	5
7 Social democratic	5.25 (1.26)	4

Figure 5.4: Child poverty/child benefit

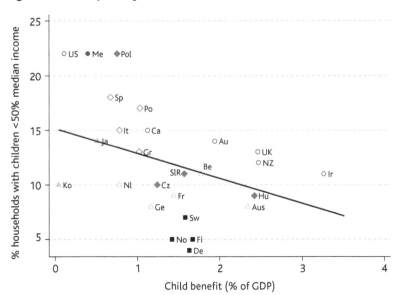

Figure 5.5: Child poverty/child services

incomes. Figure 5.5 bears witness to this, with increases in expenditure on child services associated with lower child poverty.

Social democratic countries demonstrate high levels of expenditure on child services which transcend those of other nation states by

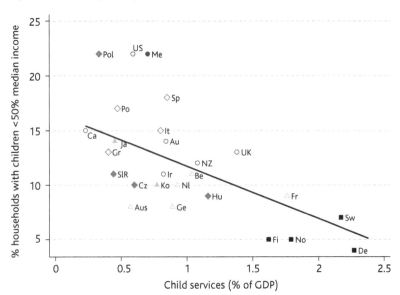

some margin, again adding to our understanding of the reasons for the lower levels of child poverty experienced. Mexico, the US and Poland have some of lowest expenditure on child benefits and services with rates of child poverty over four times those found in social democratic countries, Denmark, Finland and Norway. Further credence is added to the notion that the generosity of child services and benefits serves to reduce the extent of child poverty, through a regression of Bradshaw's measure of child support, which provides a notional figure for the generosity of child support packages (including benefit, services, care and tax benefits) with child poverty rates. This demonstrated a significant association ($p=0.003$) with incremental rises in the generosity of child support associated with falls in child poverty rates. It is important to note that, as is the case of relative poverty, a positive association is found between trust and child poverty rates ($p<0.0001$). Thus, those societies that have high levels of trust appear to have lower rates of child poverty. There would appear to be an important relationship between social solidarity and the generosity of social protection systems.

Financial insecurity

In recent years considerable sociological focus has been devoted to the precarious nature of life in contemporary capitalist societies. Fragile global financial systems and flexible labour markets, the consequences of which lie beyond the comprehension and control of many of us, serve to generate anxiety and uncertainties. Just how precarious our lives have become is debatable, but this perhaps misses the point – it is how people perceive their position in the world and the control they exert over their lives that is important, and it is exactly this injurious phenomena that this harm attempts to capture. Financial insecurity, while related to relative poverty, remains a distinct phenomena, insofar as it does not identify an income required to meet an individual's human needs; rather, it seeks to capture the precarious nature of household incomes in meeting obligations. Financial insecurity then refers to a complex process that entwines both the objective reality of fragile household finances with the perception and feelings of uncertainty arising from this situation. Indeed, this is not necessarily restricted to low-income households, or those experiencing poverty, but could also result when households are heavily indebted or work in insecure areas of the labour market. Financial insecurity results when we cannot control the constancy and certainty of our incomes – such as wages, pensions or benefits payments – to meet our financial obligations/commitments. It is this lack of control and the permanent state of anxiety over the exogenous shocks that could befall households with little or no savings or without private insurance products to safeguard against life course events, such as job loss, death of a partner or relationship breakdown, which this harm attempts to encapsulate.

Financial insecurity should be considered as autonomy harm, as it serves to undermine our capacity to formulate life strategies and ability to initiate action towards these goals due to the debilitating effect of the uncertainty and inconstancy of our of resources. As with other harms discussed in this chapter, financial insecurity gives rise to a host of secondary harms. It often generates high levels of anxiety and stress that can be predictors of poor health outcomes. As Ferrie et al (2003, p 644) found:

> Financial insecurity contributed considerably to gradients in self-rated health, longstanding illness, and depression in both employed and non-employed men, as well as to GHQ [General Health Questionnaire] score and diastolic blood pressure in non-employed men only. Adjustment for financial insecurity in non-employed women substantially attenuated gradients in self-rated health, GHQ score and depression.

It is interesting to note that Ferrie et al's analysis (2003) found a more profound impact on health when it tested financial insecurity, as opposed to a more specific measure of job insecurity. Financial insecurity gives insights into a broader sense of ontological anxiety to which job insecurity contributes, yet encompasses a more fundamental sense of a loss of control over the decisions that have an impact on our lives, that give rise to a host of deleterious secondary physical and mental health harms.

An ANOVA of the rate of financial security (log scale) on regime demonstrated strong evidence of a difference between regimes unlikely to be due to chance ($p<0.0001$). The percentage finding it difficult to live on incomes is higher in the neoliberal, post-socialist corporatist and southern corporatist regimes – it is unsurprising that the latter reported such levels of insecurity given the economic crises experienced by these nation states. The social democratic regime is significantly lower than all other six regimes (see Table 5.3).

Again, it is necessary to unpick the reasons that underlie this marked variance, and in particular, why social democratic countries have considerably lower levels of financial insecurity than other regime

Table 5.3: Financial insecurity by regime

| | % of the population finding it difficult to live on income | | Number |
Regime	Mean (SD)	Median (range)	obs
1 Neoliberal	40.00 (10.49)	42.50 (26–49)	4
2 Liberal	16.00 (2.68)	15.50 (13–21)	6
3 Post-socialist corporatist	38.83 (18.30)	36.00 (19–40)	6
4 Southern corporatist	36.25 (18.32)	29.50 (23–63)	4
5 Meso-corporatist	15.50 (4.95)	15.50 (12–19)	2
6 Northern corporatist	13.50 (3.70)	14.00 (9–17)	4
7 Social democratic	7.50 (2.38)	6.50 (6–11)	4

types. Interestingly, those nations that have lower levels of social solidarity would appear to have a higher proportion of the population finding it difficult to live on their current income, and conversely, those nation states that have high social solidarity have lower levels of financial insecurity. As Figure 5.6 demonstrates, trust ($p<0.0001$) has a positive association with lower levels of insecurity (log scale), and most notably, social democratic countries exemplify this relationship.

Inequality also demonstrates an association ($p=0.013$) insofar as those societies with greater levels of inequality have higher levels of financial insecurity. It is difficult to know for certain how social

Figure 5.6: Financial insecurity/trust

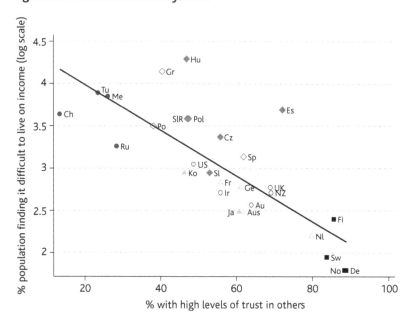

solidarity has an impact on financial insecurity. In relation to trust, as with other harms in this section, it may well be that trust provides an important underlying factor that influences other characteristics of social organisation, for example, decommodification institutions such as generous social security systems. Conversely, high levels of inequality may undermine support for these systems, as they appear to be only necessary for those who are forced to rely on them. Moreover, it may also be the case that highly unequal societies have a greater reliance on commodified forms of financial security, so that insecurity is unequally distributed throughout society, largely dependent on our ability to buy private products that insure us against the risks principally generated by the market.

Considerable academic attention has been devoted to demonstrating the precarious nature of contemporary labour markets and the influence of globalisation on this trend, or at least, the perception that work is less secure. Deregulated labour markets have an impact on job security and the value of wages. It is logical, in this context, that a safeguard against deregulation is state intervention within the labour market and trade union membership and activity. Evidence was found of an association between the strength of employment regulation and financial insecurity ($p=0.070$). In addition, trade union density demonstrated a statically significant association with financial insecurity (log scale) ($p<0.0001$). As Figure 5.7 illustrates, higher levels of trade union membership appear to be associated with lower levels of financial security. Again, social democratic countries are a distinct cluster, demonstrating in some instances double the level of membership to even corporatist countries. Within this group, Finland is, to some extent, an outlier, as it has nearly double the percentage of population experiencing financial insecurity than other social democratic regime countries, yet relatively speaking, these rates are low compared to other nation states. Nation states with low levels of union membership also vary dramatically; for example, France and Turkey have comparable rates of trade union density, but contrasting outcomes for financial insecurity.

In some respects, the differential impact of trade union membership noted above may be explained through the nature and extent of social protection expenditure. There is an association between social expenditure and financial insecurity (log scale) ($p=0.012$). As Figure 5.8 demonstrates, as social protection spending increases, insecurity appears to diminish. To some degree the aggregate expenditure masks some important associations. The first, public expenditure on social services, also appears to protect populations from financial insecurity

Figure 5.7: Financial insecurity/trade union density

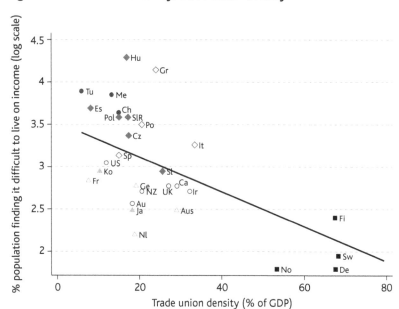

Figure 5.8: Financial insecurity/social expenditure

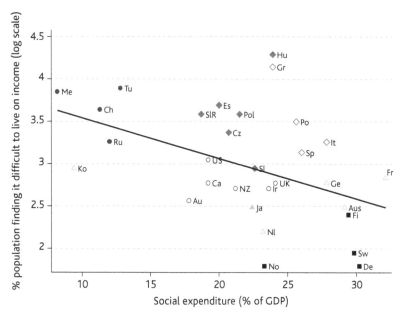

(log scale) ($p<0.0001$). It demonstrates how public services can supplement household income because such services take pressure from already stretched household budgets. Second, benefit generosity appears to also have a statistically significant association with financial insecurity (log scale) (unemployment replacement rate, $p=0.0022$). Thus, more generous benefits payments appear to be associated with lower levels of financial insecurity.

Long working hours

For many, obtaining paid work in capitalist societies is vital to their financial security and wellbeing, yet the length of the working day is rarely considered to be potentially harmful. Primarily, long working hours should be considered to be autonomy harm as the length of a working day can compromise a person's ability to lead the life of their choosing. In other words, individuals have less time to develop interests and skills outside of paid work. Moreover, long working hours can seriously compromise a person's capacity to sustain family life, as well as to form and maintain friendships. In addition, there are also a host of secondary physical and mental health harms that result from working long hours – to which the section returns below.

It is important to first establish what are considered 'long' working hours for the purposes of this analysis – which, as one would expect, given the implications for capital, is fiercely contested. The OECD appears to have adopted a definition of 'very long' working hours, that is, at <50 hours, on the basis that people working these hours would be left with 'one or two hours' a day for non-work activities, coupled with the fact that the EU Working Time Directive has sought to limit the working week to 48 hours. A review of the existing epidemiological evidence suggests that the 50-hour threshold would appear to be arbitrary. This evidence reveals that, as one might expect, the harmful impacts of working over 50 hours a week are more acute, yet the deleterious consequences of hours worked appear to manifest from 40 hours per week onwards – the latter threshold forms the basis of the following analysis.

As stated above, the available empirical evidence appears to suggest that related harms begin to accumulate when we work beyond 40 hours per week. Harms appear to increase significantly as the length of the working day increases. Thus, Artazcoz et al (2009) found that working 41-50 hours a week was related to higher levels of job dissatisfaction for both men and women, while men working these hours were more likely to adopt unhealthy behaviours – to be sedentary during leisure time and sleeping for six hours or less a day. Similar harmful outcomes were identified for men working 51-60 hours a week, who were more likely to report poor mental health status, hypertension, job dissatisfaction and no leisure time physical activity (Artazcoz et al, 2009). These findings are replicated in other studies. For example, Virtanen et al's study of British civil servants reveals 'that working 41–55 hours per week, when compared to normal working hours, was related to a 35% greater likelihood of "waking without feeling refreshed"' (2009, p 739). The tiredness and fatigue that arises from working long hours also appears to be associated with increased risks of workplace accidents in safety-critical activities. As Wagstaff and Lie found, '... work periods >8 hours carry an increased risk of accidents that cumulates, so that the increased risk of accidents at around 12 hours is twice the risk at 8 hours' (2011, p 185). Unsurprisingly, there is considerable evidence that supports the link between long working hours and poor mental health outcomes, in particular, anxiety (Kleppa et al, 2008) and depression (Shields, 1999). Virtanen et al suggest that these problems increase incrementally, with male participants demonstrating a 'linear association between each 10-h increase in working hours and the onset of anxiety symptoms' (2011, p 2489).

Harrington's review (2001) of the impacts of long working hours and shift work demonstrates a host of harmful impacts on a worker's family and social life. Thus, workers who work long hours can experience considerable disruption of family and social activities through time spent away from home, particularly through evenings and weekends. Discharging duties expected of familial roles, as a partner, parent or sibling, can be seriously disrupted by long working hours. This can place acute pressure on relationships, through inability to perform household duties in relation to 'childcare, housework, shopping ...' as well as 'leaving a partner alone at night' that can cumulatively place a strain on personal relationships (Harrington, 2001, p 69). Work at weekends can also preclude involvement in hobbies, sporting events or religious activities, which are likely to result in failure to maintain friendships and social networks, therefore increasing the possibility of marginalisation and social exclusion (Harrington, 2001).

An ANOVA regression of long working hours by regime demonstrated strong evidence of a difference between regimes unlikely to be due to chance ($p<0.0001$) (see Table 5.4). The percentage of workforce working 40+ hours was notably higher within the neoliberal, post-socialist, southern corporatist and meso-corporatist regimes than the liberal, northern corporatist and social democratic

Table 5.4: Long working hours by regime

	% of workforce working 40+ hrs	
Regime	Mean (SD)	Number obs
1 Neoliberal	76.00 (6.56)	3
2 Liberal	52.17 (14.55)	6
3 Post-socialist corporatist	86.50 (3.45)	6
4 Southern corporatist	69.75 (8.18)	4
5 Meso-corporatist	69.50 (9.19)	2
6 Northern corporatist	40.80 (11.67)	5
7 Social democratic	31.75 (21.56)	4

regimes. The social democratic regime is significantly lower than [sentence removed] all except the northern corporatist regime. Again, within regimes there are some notable outliers. Within the liberal regime, the US has twice the percentage of workforce working long hours than the UK, Australia and Canada. Similarly, Sweden has six times the proportion of its workforce working long hours compared to Denmark and Finland. Thus, the factors that lie behind individual nation states working hours must again be explored.

An obvious starting point for this analysis is to understand the balance of relations between capital and workers within each nation state. In particular, the analysis presented here seeks to examine the fetters placed on employers through workplace regulation by state regulatory bodies and trade union membership. Regressions conducted using measures of employment regulation and trade union density demonstrate strong evidence of an association between trade union density and the percentage of the workforce working over 40 hours a week ($p=0.0003$). As Figure 5.9 shows, increases in trade union membership appear to be related to corresponding falls in the percentage of the workforce working over 40 hours a week.

There are notable outliers in Figure 5.9 that are worthy of discussion. First, France has low numbers of workers working over 40 hours a week, yet relatively low levels of union membership. The relatively low proportion of the working force may be explained by the recent history of French legislation that places statutory limits on to the working week – a 35-hour week. It should be noted that exceptions apply to this legislation, and the limit applies unevenly across the workforce (Fagnani and Letablier, 2004). Second, Sweden exhibits the reverse, high union membership, yet a relatively high proportion of the Swedish workforce work over 40 hours. Traditionally, working time has been heavily influenced by collective bargaining and working

Figure 5.9: Long working hours/trade union density

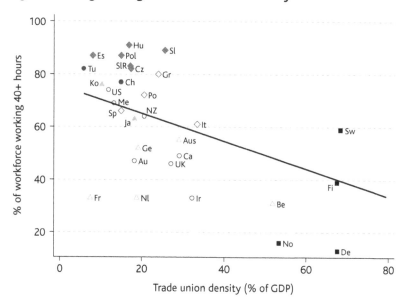

hours are limited to a statutory 40-hour week (Berg et al, 2004). Despite these measures, there is a great deal of latitude within these national agreements and legislation for local agreements to vary these conditions depending on the sector and individual circumstances of firms (Anxo, 2009). These local agreements serve to offer workers the opportunity to choose between shorter hours or pay increases through longer working days, and there is an increasing trend towards decentralisation (Anxo, 2009). In line with previous studies, however, trade union membership remains an important factor in the regulation of working hours – in particular, the influence of collective bargaining over working conditions and the importance of workplace representation that trade unions provide (Berg et al, 2004; van Wanrooy and Wilson, 2006).

Youth unemployment

It is a function of the capitalist mode of production that some of us will have too much work, while others will experience frequent episodes without paid work or, for that matter, any form of productive activity to engage in. The term NEET has relatively recently entered policy and public discourses as a means to capture young people who are neither employed or in some form of tertiary education or training. While in recent years unemployment has increased almost universally across the OECD as a result of the Great Recession, youth unemployment has increased at a greater rate than adult rates. This trend underlies a broader historical trend that predates the global economic crisis, whereby youth unemployment has increased relative to adult unemployment. The definition of NEET is not without its issues, particularly when used as an indicator of harm, as it may be assumed that any form of employment and education are prima facie positive human experiences. Nevertheless, NEET may act as a proxy indicator of harm, insofar as it captures the absence of formal opportunities to either engage in productive forms of work, skills acquisition or learning. Thus, this enforced inactivity could be viewed as autonomy harm, as it denies the necessary opportunities for self-actualisation to be realised – in the ways described above.

Indeed, the academic literature, dominated by economics, makes reference to the 'scarring' effects of youth unemployment or NEET rates. While these are largely as a result of the financial impacts, the literature also points to broader secondary psychosocial harms. The 'scarring' effects reported in studies on youth unemployment report increased risks of future unemployment in later life – mainly as a result of lost opportunities to develop skills and to accumulate sufficient levels of experience (Scarpetta et al, 2010; Bell and Blanchflower, 2011). Gregg's analysis (2001) shows that men who experience an extra three months' unemployment before the age of 23 go on to experience an additional two months out of work between the ages of 28 and 33. It is certainly not the case that episodes of unemployment have a uniform impact. Bell and Blanchflower suggest that 'unemployment while young, especially of long duration, appears to be associated with permanent scars rather than the temporary blemishes that result for older workers' (2011, p 15). The point is that older workers appear to recover more quickly from a spell of unemployment given their demonstrable employment histories, whereas unemployment is potentially more damaging for younger people who are less likely to have an established employment history, nor will they have accumulated the necessary skills and experience to gain speedy re-entry into the labour market (Bell and Blanchflower, 2011).

In terms of the 'wage penalty', numerous studies detail the impacts of periods of youth unemployment. Mroz and Savage (2006) report that a period of unemployment at the age of 22 results in an 8 per cent lower wage at 23, and this can still be felt at the ages of 30-31, with wages 2-3 per cent lower than would be expected. Moreover, Gregg and Tominey's UK study (2005) found a period of youth unemployment of one year at the age of 22, and reduced wages by 13-21 per cent

20 years later. It would appear that the initial period of unemployment is the most costly in terms of future earnings – as Arulampalam's (2001) study reports, the first spell to result in an average penalty of 10.4 per cent loss of earnings, with subsequent spells carrying a wage penalty, however, an albeit diminished one of approximately 8.7 per cent in the following spell of unemployment.

More recently, studies have sought to document the psychosocial impacts of youth unemployment. In Bell and Blanchflower's summary of the available research evidence, they identify a host of secondary mental health and relational harms that result from the experience of youth unemployment:

> ... in comparison, with other young people, the young unemployed were significantly more likely to feel ashamed, rejected, lost, anxious, insecure, down and depressed, isolated and unloved. They were also significantly less happy with their health, friendships and family life than those in work or studying, much less confident of the future and more likely to say that they had turned to drugs, that they had nothing to look forward to and that their life had no direction. Many reported having suicidal thoughts.... (Bell and Blanchflower, 2011, p 16)

In line with this evidence base, Bell and Blanchflower's primary analyses reveal that periods of youth unemployment have deleterious effects on happiness, wellbeing and job satisfaction in later life.

An ANOVA of the percentage of 20- to 24-year-olds not in education or employment (log scale) on regime demonstrated evidence of a difference between regimes unlikely to be due to chance ($p=0.0157$). The percentage not in education or employment in the neoliberal regime was dramatically higher than in the liberal, post-socialist corporatist, northern corporatist and social democratic regimes. The social democratic regime demonstrates the lowest NEET rates. It is important to note the high NEET rates in the southern corporatist regimes – a result of the economic crisis and austerity measures undertaken in these nation states. A similar pattern is demonstrated when an ANOVA of the percentage of 15- to 19-year-olds not in education or employment (log scale) on regime is performed, which also demonstrated evidence of a difference between regimes unlikely to be due to chance ($p=0.0001$).

Unpicking the contrasting performance of regimes again relies on exploring the individual characteristics of societies in relation to key

Table 5.5: NEETS by regime

Regime	% of 20 to 24-year-olds not in education or employment		Number obs
	Mean (SD)	Median (range)	
1 Neoliberal	35.15 (12.09)	35.15 (26.60–43.70)	2
2 Liberal	17.98 (4.41)	18.85 (11.20–24.30)	6
3 Post-socialist corporatist	17.77 (5.35)	19.60 (9.30–22.40)	6
4 Southern corporatist	23.13 (5.22)	24.35 (16.40–27.40)	4
5 Meso-corporatist	23.50	23.5	1
6 Northern corporatist	14.54 (4.96)	13.70 (7.80–20.60)	5
7 Social democratic	12.80 (2.95)	13.20 (9.00–15.80)	4

Regime	% of 15 to 19-year-olds not in education or employment		Number obs
	Mean (SD)	Median (range)	
1 Neoliberal	22.10 (4.95)	22.10 (18.60–25.60)	2
2 Liberal	9.12 (1.28)	9.10 (7.60–10.40)	6
3 Post-socialist corporatist	4.32 (1.04)	4.20 (3.20–6.10)	6
4 Southern corporatist	9.23 (3.09)	7.50 (7.40–12.80)	3
5 Meso-corporatist	9.20 (0.99)	9.80 (8.50–9.90)	2
6 Northern corporatist	5.90 (2.15))	5.90 (3.70–8.20)	5
7 Social democratic	4.88 (0.93)	5.25 (3.50–5.50)	4

determining factors of harm. In terms of youth unemployment, the existing literature identifies risk factors that render young people vulnerable in general to unemployment, as well as specific groups. Generally, youth unemployment appears to be shaped by young people's educational experience and qualifications, but also their disproportionate presence in the most insecure segments of the labour market (Gregg, 2001; Scarpetta et al, 2010). In the analyses presented here, these factors appear to go some way to explain the differences between nation states and regimes in relation to NEET rates. Beginning with education, regressions performed demonstrate statistically significant associations between education spending and the level of NEET for 15- to 19-year-olds ($p=0.031$) and 20- to 24-year-olds ($p=0.002$). Thus the more that nation states appear to spend on public education, the lower the levels of NEET (log scale). To some extent it is self-evident that greater public expenditure on education would raise the possibility that greater numbers of young people would remain within education for longer and, ultimately, lower NEET rates. Yet the available literature assists our understanding of this relationship, particularly in relation to youth unemployment. As

Scarpetta et al's analysis of youth unemployment in the OECD reveals, the 'employment rate of youth aged 15-29 having left education with a tertiary diploma is higher than the employment rate of those with an upper secondary diploma, which is in turn higher than that of those with no diploma, except in Italy...' (2010, p 16). Moreover, they observe that in many contemporary labour markets, obtaining an upper secondary education qualification has become a minimum expectation of many employers, thus those leaving school without such a qualification are immediately placed at a disadvantage (Scarpetta et al, 2010).

A common theme within the literature on youth unemployment suggests that young people are disproportionately located within more precarious forms of work. As Scarpetta et al observe, 'the incidence of temporary employment among young workers aged 15-24 was 35% in 2008 on average in the OECD area, an increase of almost 5 percentage points since 1998' (2010, p 17). It follows that the relative strength and comprehensiveness of labour market regulation would serve to safeguard young people from the vulnerability of temporary work. Regression conducted on NEET and employment regulation burden did not provide a statistically significant association – this may be because the employment regulation burden is a general measure, not specific to young people, so does not capture the exemption clauses in many nation states' employment protection legislation that leave young people more vulnerable than older workers. However, there is evidence from previous studies that these labour market regulations make it easier to terminate young workers' contracts of employment (Bell and Blanchflower, 2011). It is interesting to note in Arulampalam's (2001) study, that where young employees were covered by legislation that requires employers to issue a notice period to the termination of contracts, the 'scarring' impact of unemployment was significantly reduced. Due to the fact that they had opportunities to begin job searches to find appropriate work, as well as the receipt of redundancy payments or being able to claim benefits without disqualification, this softened the blow to young people's incomes.

It is worth noting, however, that NEET and trade union density demonstrate some evidence of an association – as Figure 5.10 highlights, those countries with higher levels of trade union membership appearing to demonstrate lower rates of NEET (20- to 24-year-olds) ($p=0.039$). It should be noted that this association was not found for 15- to 19-year-olds ($p=0.101$).

Trade union density is an important contextual factor – insofar as these rates give us an insight into the extent to which young workers

Figure 5.10: NEETS/trade union density

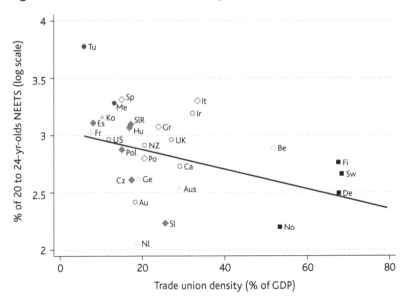

may be protected by workplace representation or may indirectly benefit from the forms of employment regulation that unions promote and the challenges they offer to casualisation. Whereas neoliberal analyses often present arguments that suggest that unions raise young workers' wages to a level where they become uncompetitive, 'pricing out' these workers, these findings would suggest otherwise. Moreover, this assertion is supported by Bell and Blanchflower's analysis (2011) that suggests that a number of societies that have high levels of youth unemployment have low youth trade union membership density rates. They are led to conclude that 'it does not appear that youths are pricing themselves out of work, unless their relative productivity is falling especially sharply, but there is no evidence to suggest this' (2011, pp 13-14).

A further factor that may add to the complexity of the analysis presented here relates to the relationship exhibited between social solidarity and contrasting NEET rates. Regression of inequality and NEET rates demonstrated evidence of an association, so that those societies with the greatest levels of inequality demonstrated higher NEET rates (log scale) ($p=0.0002$). Conversely, regression of trust and NEET rates demonstrates a negative association, so that those societies reporting high levels of trust in others appear to have lower levels of NEET (log scale) ($p=0.0001$). It would appear that societies that exhibit greater levels of social solidarity have lower rates of NEET.

Explaining this apparent association is not necessarily straightforward; nevertheless, it does not appear to be illogical to suggest that, again, this provides important contextual information that points to the importance of collective responses to harm. In relation to NEET, while levels of youth unemployment in more fractured societies may be viewed as the result of personal failure or the subcultural rejection of work, more solidaristic societies are perhaps likely to view these rates as a product of structural forces. Thus, the latter societies exhibit greater collective support for the increased educational spending and employment regulation that serve to reduce the NEET rates in these societies.

Social isolation

Social isolation is a growing concern within late capitalist societies. It is viewed as largely the problem of ageing populations resulting from the advancement of healthcare in many societies – ironically, the extension of life expectancy appears to beget other harms (Findlay, 2003). As Dickens et al note, in the UK 'people aged 60 or above currently account for approximately 20% of the population and this proportion is expected to rise to 24% by 2030 ... [i]n comparison, 11% of the world's population was aged 60 or above in 2007, rising to an estimated 22% by 2050' (2011, p 648). Moreover, as House et al predict, this is not a problem that is likely to diminish in many societies unless it is confronted, as '...changes in marital and childbearing patterns and in the age structure ... will produce a steady increase of the number of older people who lack spouses or children – the people to whom older people most often turn for relatedness and support' (1988, p 544). While old age undoubtedly creates vulnerability to isolation and may be the key determining factor, it should also be noted that other groups are also vulnerable in this regard, such as lone parents, and those living on low incomes. It may also be that the levels of isolation currently experienced are symptomatic of our increasingly individualised societies.

Social isolation, as an enforced condition, is without doubt an injurious state of being – as human beings we are social creatures requiring companionship and kinship relations in order to flourish. Aside from the psychosocial injury derived from existing outside of social networks, there is clear empirical evidence that demonstrates the collateral harms associated with isolation. There is a considerable evidence base that demonstrates the negative impacts of isolation on health; for instance, a recent review of 148 longitudinal studies conducted by Holt-Lunstad et al (2010) discovered a 50 per cent reduction in the likelihood of mortality for individuals with strong social relationships. Aside from the association between social isolation and increased mortality, as Dickens et al summarise (2011), studies have identified the relationship between social isolation and a host of poor health outcomes, including low levels of self-rated physical health, increased susceptibility to dementia and the onset of disability for older men. House et al note the irony, as epidemiological research has come to fully understand 'the importance of social relationships for health ... as their prevalence and availability may be declining...' (1988, p 544); they continue to suggest that as 'changes in other risk factors (for example, the decline of smoking) and improvements in medical technology are still producing overall improvements on health and longevity, but the improvements might be even greater if the quantity and quality of social relationships were also improving' (p 544).

While there is contestation within the literature, primarily gerontology literature, over the definition of social isolation and its interrelationship with loneliness, this section draws on a definition offer by Wenger et al (1996, p 333):

> ... the objective state of having minimal contact with other
> people; while loneliness refers to the subjective state of
> negative feelings associated with perceived social isolation,
> a lower level of contact than that desired or the absence of
> a specific desired companion.

In line with Wenger et al's 'objective' definition of social isolation, a measure of 'not seeing friends within last year' is used as a proxy in the analyses for this section. An ANOVA of the percentage of those not seeing friends in the last year found no evidence of significant differences between regimes ($p=0.220$), but this may have been due to small numbers of nations for which data is available. However, it would appear that social democratic nation states exhibit lower rates of isolation according to this measure, with little difference demonstrated between the other regimes (see Table 5.6 opposite).

Given the lack of statistical significance and the difficulties associated with drawing inference in variation between regimes, it is important to compare the variance in rates against key structural features of these societies to explain the tentative observations made above. Inequality, when regressed with social isolation, demonstrated a positive statistically significant association, insofar as societies that exhibit high levels of inequality tend to have higher levels of social

Table 5.6: Social isolation by regime

Regime	% not seeing friends within last year Mean (SD)	Number obs
1 Neoliberal		0
2 Liberal	11.50 (0.71)	2
3 Post-socialist corporatist	10.33 (4.37)	6
4 Southern corporatist	14.00 (8.49)	4
5 Meso-corporatist		0
6 Northern corporatist	11.00 (3.16)	5
7 Social democratic	5.75 (1.26)	4

isolation ($p=0.006$). Perhaps this is unsurprising given the body of work on inequality that demonstrates the fragmented nature of highly unequal societies (Wilkinson and Pickett, 2010). In part, this may go some way to explain the lower levels of isolation experienced within the social democratic regime, given the low rates of inequality found in these countries (see Figure 5.11).

Similarly, expenditure on public services appears to demonstrate an association with social isolation ($p=0.033$). Thus, societies that have relatively high levels of public service expenditure exhibit lower rates of isolation. Again, social democratic regimes exhibit the highest level of social service expenditure, and consequently, the lowest rates of isolation. Services would appear to be important factors in protecting

Figure 5.11: Social isolation/inequality

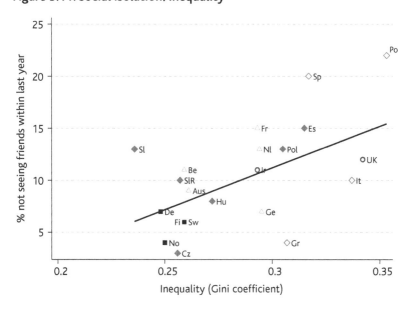

populations from social isolation. As existing research reveals, factors that appear to contribute to social isolation include bereavement, poor physical health, mental illness, low esteem, being a carer, and geographic location. Wenger et al (1996, pp 345-6) conclude that many factors that serve to isolate individuals are beyond their control and are 'not obviously susceptible to amelioration'. However, it is logical that services that support communities through maintaining social contacts and networks for vulnerable populations, such as those with mental illness or limiting illness/disability, carers and rural populations without access to transport, serve to ameliorate the individualising tendencies of contemporary capitalist societies.

Conclusion

Capitalist societies celebrate the liberties and freedoms they bestow on their populations. Yet, as the analysis in this chapter demonstrates, the ways in which capitalist societies are organised serve to habitually compromise human autonomy, often through the exercise of individual freedoms within the market. Similarly, the individualism and self-interest that drives capitalist wealth accumulation and permeates many aspects of social life frustrates our ability to be with others, driving the corrosive fragmentation of communities, leaving many isolated. Despite the fact that these are arguably uniform features of capitalism, the production of these harms, as this chapter demonstrates, vary considerably.

As with Chapter Four, the data present a complex picture, with nation states at times demonstrating contrasting and contradictory levels of performance in relation to specific autonomy and relational harms. Nevertheless, a pattern begins to emerge in relation to the regimes and autonomy and relational harms analysed here. The neoliberal regimes demonstrate consistently higher levels of autonomy and relational harms – notably, the southern corporatist regime also demonstrated high levels of harm, which may be explained in part by the crises that have engulfed these societies. The northern corporatist and social democratic regimes have consistently lower levels of autonomy and relational harm. With the liberal regime and remainder corporatist regimes, it is more difficult to discern such clear aggregate patterns of harm production – with the exception of specific nation states such as the US.

The analyses presented here, as with the previous empirical chapter, has proposed a series of factors that seek to explain why some societies are able to organise themselves in such a way to militate against the production of these harms. The chapter concludes by drawing together these analyses to pass general comment on the aspects of social organisation that prove to be generative or reduce the extent of autonomy and relational harms.

First, as with physical harms, societies that demonstrate high levels of *decommodification* seem better equipped to protect their populations against autonomy and relational harms. Thus, societies that have relatively generous forms of social security and extensive social services tend to provide resources and opportunities independent of an individual's position within the market, and in doing so, militate against the production of autonomy harms. Moreover, decommodification provides the means and opportunities to sustain our position in social networks, and to avoid the individualising impacts of capitalist organisation.

Second, *trustful societies* demonstrate a high degree of social solidarity, and this appears to support harm reduction features – in particular, decommodification. The nature of this relationship is not entirely clear, and it requires further consideration, insofar as it is certainly not the case that one simply causes the other, but that there is a dialectic relation that material practices of decommodification inspire solidaristic societal forms, and these guarantee the ideological grounds that ensure decommodification continues in one guise or another.

Finally, *fettering capital*, particularly in the extraction of surplus value, is critical to the amelioration of autonomy harms – in terms of improving the value of wages, the security of work and working conditions. Trade unions appear to play a fundamental role in this process, alongside state regulatory mechanisms that serve to mediate the worst excesses of the exploitation of wage labour.

SIX

Harm reduction regimes, neoliberalism and the production of harm

This, the final chapter, seeks to consolidate and extend the thematic and empirical strands that have run through the book up to this point, to reach a series of concluding, albeit tentative, thoughts on the production of harm in capitalist societies. It therefore begins by revisiting the social harm 'lens' to reflect on its merits and limitations. In doing so, it specifically assesses the ability of this lens to capture the interwoven and interrelated nature of harms within capitalist society.

However, this chapter principally serves to complete the trajectory of the twin themes of 'preventable harm' and the 'variance of capitalist harm' that run throughout the analysis. In a way, the analysis provided in the book lends itself to a regime 'contest' in which regimes have been evaluated in respect of their performance according to a number of harm indicators, and we therefore eventually arrive at a conclusion over the 'best' and 'worst' harm reduction regimes. Developing the analyses provided in Chapters Four and Five, this chapter draws together the observations made thus far, to explain how the features of these regimes determine the contrasting levels of harms between societies. The analysis is further developed through the examination of outliers within regimes that deviate significantly from the norms of the regime family. Such an exercise aids our understanding of the ways in which different aspects of harm reduction interrelate and shape the forms that these regimes take – providing a more holistic sense of harm prevention. Not only does this analysis allow reflection on the aspects of social organisation that serve to generate or reduce harms, but further contributes to the argument that these harms are preventable, insofar as they do not appear to conform to a 'natural' rate, as specific forms of organisation demonstrably 'design out' harms from societies.

It is important to add a significant caveat at this point, that the judgements made in this chapter in relation to 'more or less' harmful capitalist forms are contingent on a number of factors. It is difficult to draw definitive conclusions on the basis of the limited number of harms reviewed in the book, and the restrictions placed on the analyses of these harms due to the paucity and availability of comparative indicators against which harms could be measured. Moreover, what prima facie might appear to be less 'harmful' may not be the case; harm may be 'hidden' insofar as its causal path remains unknown or contested. For instance, advanced industrialised societies may demonstrate lower occupational harms and falling rates of physical injury, yet this statistical 'trend' may obscure the deaths caused by occupational diseases, such as cancers resulting from exposure to chemicals or stress that results some time after initial exposure, and therefore remains undetected by official data sources. In addition, advanced industrialised economies are likely to 'displace' harms or 'relocate harm production' rather than design it out. For instance, through the development of global chains of production, where capital in search of lower production costs has relocated to deregulated low-waged labour markets in the developing world, hazardous work conditions, excessive working hours and bonded labour have been extensively documented within these production chains. Thus, any historic trends or geographical variation in harm production must be treated with these caveats in mind.

The chapter concludes with an assessment of the role of the social harm lens in the 'post-crisis' conjuncture of 'resurgent' neoliberalism. Social harm has been accused of being an inherently negative discourse (Muncie, 2000); this book has done little to debunk this notion, providing an analysis of the unremitting human misery caused by capitalist harms, allied to the prospect that neoliberalism's ascendancy will only generate further harm. Yet Chapter Two sought to argue that the concept of social harm should be informed by a utopian desire to articulate the possibility of less harmful forms of social organisation. This chapter finishes by considering how a social harm analysis, such as the one presented in the book, may contribute to the development of successful transformative critiques.

Developing a more systematic lens?

The intention of the book was to outline what a social harm lens might look like, and the forms of analysis that it can contribute to understanding the production of capitalist harm. Naturally, the usual caveats apply, insofar as any 'grand narrative' is constrained by the contingencies of what remains 'humanly possible', yet given the nature of the conjuncture, there is an urgent need for a 'lens' to promote critique of the injurious developments, however inadequately formulated. Purposefully broad, the lens is based on a triad of ontological properties necessary for human flourishing – a level of physical and mental health that allows successful human action; the capacity for autonomous action in order to lead lives of our own choosing; and sustaining human relations that afford us the ability to be with others. Thus, the lens presented here identifies specific harms that result when human flourishing is compromised in these three forms. Inevitably such a broad definition means that seemingly diverse and distinct harms have been presented alongside one another. Although prima facie it may appear to be incoherent, it is important that social harm analyses do not present harms in isolation, as hermetically sealed analytical spaces that abstract harm from the social contexts in which they exist. Thus, considerable effort was devoted in Chapters Four and Five to understanding how harms relate to one another, and to highlight the synergistic and cumulative impacts of harms across the life course.

In particular, the examination of autonomy and relational harms in Chapter Five reveals a host of secondary physical/mental health harms. By examining these phenomena alongside one another we are able to begin to piece together an overarching narrative of the many injurious ways that human potential is frustrated and compromised by capitalist society. Thus, a more rounded picture emerges of harmful societies. Many who have work in capitalist societies are likely to work long hours that allow little time to sustain meaningful social relations, to exercise, enjoy hobbies or leisure time, or to sustain healthy lifestyles, and, therefore, they are more likely to experience health problems, including heart disease and depressive and anxiety disorders. Yet for those who do not have work, for example, those experiencing periods of youth unemployment, enforced periods of economic inactivity have serious injurious consequences for their future financial security, as well as the psychosocial injuries that have an impact on self-esteem and perception of self-worth. Similarly, the experience of child poverty is likely to have a deleterious impact on a person's ability to develop particular skills and cognitive abilities that determine future opportunities and choices. For those who experience periods of poverty in adulthood, as well as restricting the ability to live lives of their choosing, they are more likely to experience social isolation and to endure mental health conditions, such as anxiety and depression; ultimately, the inability to lead healthy lifestyles due to a lack of resources foreshortens lives.

The lens presented here makes possible seemingly unconnected social events that too often defy the bounded disciplinary specialisms of contemporary social science. It is rare that social science analyses attempt to draw connections between the varied injurious characteristics of our societies. Moreover, the analyses presented have drawn on a diverse and broad empirical literature, notably from epidemiology, criminology, social policy, geography, economics and psychology. Through combining a variety of disciplinary lenses into one, we are able to achieve a more rounded understanding of the ways that human flourishing are compromised, lending a degree of credence to the notion that 'social harm' as a field of study can develop truly multidisciplinary lens(es). The use of the plural here is important. The book has presented a 'version' of the social harm approach, which is not intended to be definitive, but rather acts as a device through which future approaches may develop. This work provides a resource that encourages critique, contestation and refinement, from which alternative approaches take hold that promote a field engaged in a relentless search for the most systematic and objective lens possible.

Before moving to discuss the findings of the book, a further caveat must be added to the approach that has been adopted here. It could be argued that the needs-based approach on which this 'lens' is based falls foul of methodological individualism that might seem to be a contradiction, given the emphasis on collective forms of harm reduction within the analyses presented. Indeed the 'lens' developed in Chapter Two is based, to some extent, on an 'abstract individual', and this raises issues for the social harm approach. It tends to identify harms at an individual level, and has the potential to omit those that occur at a collective level – more specifically, harms that can be inflicted on social groups and the injurious states that result when the social fabric which knits together individuals is damaged. Yet the relational harm category purposefully attempts to capture the harms that result from the injuries that are inflicted on the 'organism' that is society – albeit these injuries are realised at the individual level. Neither does the 'ontological' reasoning that stems from the 'abstract individual' necessarily result in an ironic celebration of individualism whereby a non-harmful state equates to unfettered individual freedom to self-actualise. The 'harm-free' society – however inadequately conceived – is based on a notion of relative autonomy where individuals flourish in ways that they choose, and have the necessary resources and opportunities to do so, but flourishing is only ever fully realised through collaboration with others. 'Collaborative flourishing' stands in stark contrast to the 'competitive flourishing' that capitalist society serves to reify, and that is predicated on the harmful exploitation and immiseration of others.

Capitalist harm: varieties of harm production?

Up to this point, the portrayal of capitalist harm in the book presents a contradictory picture: harm as a feature common to all capitalist societies, yet varying in extent according to the specific form societies take. While much of the analysis presented in Chapters Four and Five highlights variance in the extent of these harms, it is also clear that capitalist organisation generates mass harms common to all societies. In particular, these analyses demonstrate how the extraction of surplus value, the experience of alienation and the relentless commodification of human relations serve to compromise human flourishing in many harmful ways. Viewed in this way, we come to see harms not as aberrations, but as a necessary feature of the capitalist system. In short, it is important to remind ourselves that while levels of capitalist harm are not a given, no matter how capitalist societies are configured, we cannot design out harms that are a fundamental feature of the functioning of capitalist systems. This does not render invalid the 'varieties of capitalist harm' thesis; rather, it defines its limitations – a point that is further developed in the final section of the chapter. Moreover, the 'varieties of capitalist harm' thesis speaks to the immediate concerns of the current conjuncture, the post-crisis neoliberal resurgence, and the mass harms that have unfolded as a consequence.

The 'varieties of capitalist harm' thesis proposed here is forged through an historical account that narrates an albeit stylised account of the emergence of more humane forms of capitalism that develop across the 20th century. From the social wreckage of chaotic and unregulated 19th-century laissez-faire capitalism and the failure of the 'patches' of social liberalism that unravelled in the wake of the 1920s 'Great Depression', emerged an era of embedded liberalism that took hold in many advanced industrialised economies. The convergence of capitalist crisis and the production of mass harms, alongside the rise of social forces, namely, organised labour and the democratic franchise, gave expression to demands for more humane capitalist forms. Many advanced capitalist societies arguably evolved into less harmful modes of organisation than had hitherto existed, through the numerous variations of embedded liberalism that took hold. The evolution of the 'social state' at this point – the mass of harm reduction infrastructure (for example, social security; public healthcare systems; public utilities; regulatory agencies; employment and trade union rights) brought about a less volatile capitalist form, and served to ameliorate, to some extent, the production of capitalist harms. This represents a rather stylised historic picture that neglects the harms that the 'social state' and 'embedded liberalism' were built on. For instance, in the post-war period, the development of services and healthcare systems in many advanced industrial economies relied heavily on the exploitation of labour drawn from the colonies, as well as the gendered stratification and the servicing of male labour on which the emergent social security systems and insurance schemes were based. Nevertheless, it remains that in relation to the harms reviewed in this book, 'embedded liberalism' in many nation states represented a less harmful capitalist form than had existed previously.

As Harvey has argued, detailed in Chapter Three, neoliberalism is best viewed as a class project that sought to reverse the more equitable patterns of income and wealth distribution, as well as opportunities, achieved in many advanced nation states in the name of 'embedded liberalism'. The point is that the variety of neoliberal projects that have taken hold since the 1970s have sought to establish the primacy of markets as mechanisms for social progress and to re-establish conditions conducive to wealth accumulation – yet the various forms of restructuring and statecraft that this has entailed have arguably had a profound impact on the systems, structures and social agreements that ensured that capitalist forms were less injurious in nature. Thus, as the neoliberal project has unfolded, those aspects of harm protection systems that are perceived to place fetters on accumulative practices have been contested, reconfigured or dismantled. Viewed in this way, the social transformation that has taken place, the reversal of gains made under 'embedded liberalism', has resulted in a series of collateral social harms. Of course not all nation states and regimes follow this historical trajectory – particularly the post-socialist countries. That said, under the communist regime in many countries, while political rights were seriously circumscribed, models of social citizenship informed the design and delivery of important services – particularly health and social security – that served to protect populations against particular physical and autonomy harms. While the transformations that took place in many communist systems brought formal civil and political freedom, the 'shock' doctrine neoliberal reforms undertaken in many stripped away many structures that served to protect. Thus, the transformation to capitalism, and often in a highly neoliberal form, led to the production of numerous harms – particularly in the case of the Russian Federation (Nesvetailova, 2005; Klein, 2007).

The analyses presented in the book have sought to contribute to an understanding of the harmful nature of the rise of neoliberalism, and the impact this has had on the existing harm reduction features of advanced industrial societies. It is not possible to provide analyses that contrast the harms generated during the era of 'embedded liberalism' with those produced as a result of 'neoliberalism'. Quite simply, suitable comparative time series data does not exist for the harms included in the book, which would enable such comparison. Thus, conclusions that suggest that 'neoliberalism' is more injurious than 'embedded liberalism' as a form of capitalist organisation cannot be made here. Rather, the cross-sectional analysis provided attempts to highlight the extent to which neoliberalism has come to be embedded within particular nation states, and how this has had an impact on the variance in the experience of harms. It is, in many respects, a more nuanced analysis, acknowledging the reality that a multiplicity of very different neoliberal projects has taken hold within distinct capitalist formations, and, therefore, the varied levels of harm may reflect the 'depth' of neoliberalism in practice.

The 'harm regimes hypothesis' proposed in Chapter Three suggests that where neoliberalism has become most deeply embedded, it has been most destructive. Yet the point is not only to focus here on the advent of neoliberalism, but also to understand how existing varieties of capitalism have an impact on the experience of social harms. It was speculated that regimes would conform to a continuum that ran from the most to the least harmful, and that those regimes that gravitated towards the more harmful end would have followed neoliberalism more closely, and have less developed harm reduction systems. Thus, it follows that those regimes that demonstrate more humane and socialised versions of capitalism, where it is more difficult for neoliberalism to become embedded, will be less harmful forms. The evidence presented in Chapters Four and Five appear to support the 'harm regimes hypothesis', insofar as the neoliberal regime, the regime that is closest to delivering the ideological model of the 'free market/minimal social state/strong state' form, appears to be the most harmful, whereas the most socialised form of regime is the least harmful. However, there are important empirical nuances that deserve greater attention that somewhat complicate this rather simplistic picture. These will now be addressed through a discussion of each regime in turn, moving from the most to the least harmful.

In seven out of the nine available measures, the neoliberal regime was the most harmful regime type. There are obvious caveats that should be considered, however, the most important of which relates to the relative GDP of nation states within this family. Thus, the ability to fund particular harm reduction technologies and services would naturally be more limited. Yet the historical trajectory is very different to other regimes, insofar as they have directly experienced either an intense period of 'neoliberal' shock therapy that recast these societies into this capitalist form, or have been radically restructured through trade agreements or financial support packages from the international agencies. It is not surprising that neoliberalism became embedded in these societies, as all have histories as strong or authoritarian states, with suppressed or fledgling democratic political cultures, and are arguably perfect host systems for the neoliberal model. If we accept that harm reduction systems arise from hegemonic agreement, and represent concessions fought for and secured through democratic channels, strong states are rarely required to make such concessions, as consent is achieved through coercive mechanisms. This provides a terrain whereby the support necessary to develop and sustain harm reduction systems does not exist. Thus, strong states are well positioned to dismantle and reconfigure harm reduction systems that place fetters on markets and capital – which serves to explain the harms produced by these forms.

There are four regimes, then, that have little to discern between them: the liberal, the post-socialist, southern corporatist and meso-corporatist. They perform differently in relation to different harms, yet fill the middle ground between the most harmful and least harmful regimes. The liberal regime demonstrates high levels of harm, and therefore performs relatively poorly, particularly considering the wealth of these nations. Except for suicide, the liberal regime is consistently in the top four most harmful regimes, according to the measures used here. This, to some extent, masks the fact that the US, on seven out of the ten available harm measures, was among the most harmful of the nations included in the analyses, and almost without exception had higher levels of harm than fellow members of the liberal regime. The US exhibited many features in harm reduction that are actually closer to those exhibited in the neoliberal regimes, in particular, high levels of inequality, low levels of social expenditure and low levels of trade unionism. The remaining nations are less extreme in nature. To varying degrees, Ireland, the UK, Australia, New Zealand and Canada tend to gravitate towards the corporatist regimes' harm reduction features.

Post-socialist societies' performance varies dramatically according to type of harm. For physical harms, this regime tends to have high levels of harm, except for road traffic injuries. However, in relation to autonomy harms, it appears to perform well, with the exception of long working hours. As with the liberal regime, one nation state appears to be a regular outlier in relation to this regime – Estonia – which, just as the US, exhibits features closer to the neoliberal regime.

The southern corporatist regime most notably demonstrates high levels of harm for the autonomy and relational harms. Having examined the limited data available that encompasses the immediate aftermath of the credit crunch as well as the initial phases of the Eurozone crisis, it would appear that the impacts of these events have led to a series of collateral harms – specifically in relation to rises in relative poverty, NEETS and financial insecurity. Thus, as austerity programmes unfold in many of these countries, and the dismantling of harm reduction systems such as social security and public healthcare, these policies will undoubtedly cause further injury to populations within this regime.

The meso-corporatist regime is difficult to assess, consisting of just two countries. While it is not possible to draw firm conclusions, this regime offers some important points in relation to corporatism as a social form. Meso-corporatism in particular reifies the importance of the 'group' rather than the individual. In one sense this creates particularly solidaristic and cohesive societies; however, the symbolic power of the 'group' and the loyalty it can generate can also be harmful. This would appear to be demonstrated by the high rates of suicide and long working hours that this regime appears to generate that result from either shame generated by 'letting down' the group, or loyalty demanded by the collective.

The northern corporatist regime, the least harmful of the corporatist forms, is consistently the second least harmful regime according to the harm measures used in Chapters Four and Five. It exhibits many similarities to the social democratic regime; however, most notably the northern corporatist regime diverges from the social democratic, as it has comparatively lower levels of trade union membership and lower expenditure on social services.

Without doubt, the least harmful regime is the social democratic regime. There is only one harm, suicide (due to Finland's high rates), where the regime is neither the least (or second least) harmful. Prima facie, the social democratic regime is distinguishable in terms of its harm reduction features, particularly in relation to high levels of social expenditure, high trade union membership, low levels of inequality and high levels of trust. With this in mind, what is it about, to some extent the northern corporatist regime, but more crucially the social democratic regime, that make these forms seemingly less harmful societies?

Harmful societies ... and less harmful capitalist societies?

The analyses presented in the book have built towards identifying the features of societies that make them more or less harmful capitalist forms. It goes without saying that a single analysis could only ever reveal partial insights into the structures and relations that protect or serve to minimise harms. In part, these limitations result from those that plague any academic endeavour, as well as the methodological approach that demands caution – as Chapter Three suggests, the associations between harms and structure must be treated as such, and not read as causation. Nevertheless, the recurring patterns and corroborative evidence presented repeatedly point to particular facets of social democratic societies (and, to a lesser extent, northern corporatist societies) that serve to reduce the production of capitalist harms, and are worthy of further exploration. In the following, an attempt is made to distil the aspects of these societies that appear to have a significant impact on the levels of capitalist harm experienced, as well as to identify features of societies – particularly the neoliberal regime – that serve to be harm generative.

Solidaristic societies

Solidaristic societies that exhibited high levels of trust and low levels of inequality appear to perform better in relation to many of the harms identified in the empirical analyses. Solidarity plays an important role in protecting populations from harm for a number of reasons. First, on an interpersonal level, those societies that have higher levels of solidarity also demonstrate greater levels of respect for others. Conversely, societies that are dramatically unequal prove to be the generative contexts for interpersonal harms, such as homicide, where *fragmented societies* exhibit higher levels of harm. It follows that in societies that have greater levels of inequality, they serve to dehumanise and devalue human life to such an extent that violence becomes a tolerated aspect of everyday life. Second, solidarity ensures greater levels of empathy for others, and militates against producing 'bystanders to harm'. Thus, solidaristic societies are likely to produce the support necessary to create and sustain harm reduction systems, more so than those that are heavily individualistic. It follows, then, that *fragmented societies* are likely to generate greater societal 'indifference' or 'passivity' towards harm, and this serves to undermine the support necessary to build harm reduction institutions.

It is interesting to note that autonomy harms appear to occur in greater frequency in individualised rather than collectivist forms of capitalist society. Individualism appears to come at a price insofar as the individual freedoms exercised by some, and often the few, come at the expense of the many. In other words, solidarity may not be the antithesis of autonomy and freedom that neoliberalism purports it to be. A caveat should be added here in regard to the harm reduction properties of solidaristic societies. Such societies tend to be bound together through high levels of social conformity and loyalty to the 'group'. Therefore, the feelings of loyalty that such societies generate can serve to produce a host of harms, when individuals are made to feel or perceive that they have not discharged their responsibility towards the 'group'. Thus marginalisation is more sharply felt in such societies, one such example being the high suicide rates in Japan and Korea.

Individualistic societies that reify competition and the unfettered enjoyment of freedom demonstrate greater levels of social disorganisation. Greater degrees of social chaos ensue when numerous individual atoms pursue their own interests with little regard to the unforeseen injurious consequences of their (in)actions or decisions. *Chaotic societies are harmful societies*, as the relatively unfettered exercise of freedom not only granted through the market, but also in all aspects of social life, such as workplaces, healthcare, education and public spaces, can have a host of injurious consequences. Road traffic deaths are an example of this, insofar as motorised travel is often viewed in capitalist society as the ultimate expression of individual freedom, yet the unfettered exercise of this freedom is incredibly harmful. Therefore those societies that have sought to limit the speed of motorised vehicles through road design, law enforcement and education appear to be able to organise urban spaces in particular that reduce road traffic deaths. Thus, even with harms that appear to be quintessentially individual in nature, societies that are willing to organise themselves to militate against the chaos of unfettered individualism serve to reduce harms.

Decommodified societies

Decommodified societies serve to recognise the worth of human beings as distinct from the contributions they make to wealth accumulation, and consequently succeed in restricting the production of capitalist harm. Decommodifcation often refers to the ability of individuals to exist within a capitalist society independent of services and wages provided through market structures. The analyses in Chapters Four and Five suggest that social spending on social security, healthcare, education and services are important harm reduction features. In crude terms, those societies that appear to have developed more universal and generous welfare systems perform better in relation to a number of harms, not only those autonomy harms, as we might intuitively expect, but also physical harms, such as infant mortality, homicide and so on. In terms of autonomy harms, it follows that those societies that pursue more vigorously principles of positive liberty, and in doing so seek to address the maldistribution of opportunities and resources that inevitably occur in capitalist societies, provide a context in which people have greater freedom to follow their life choices.

It should be noted that where the social democratic regime stands in stark contrast to the other regimes in this study is the level of expenditure and commitment to public services. From the analysis conducted, services appear to be key to protecting populations from harm. Services alleviate social problems, thus an extensive range of mental health services and addiction services can have a major impact on crime, suicide, and poor health outcomes. In addition, services facilitate social relations, they provide the context in which informal networks can be fostered and contact with others established, which is important, particularly for preventing harms of social isolation, but also in terms of building social capital that serve to militate against other harms, such as poverty, unemployment and so on.

In addition, *decommodified societies* are more likely to make available harm reduction technologies that would otherwise only be available through market mechanisms. The point is, that while advanced industrial economies purport, through the investment and innovation that wealth accumulation encourages, to develop technologies that have a significant impact on harm reduction systems, without the requisite structures they cannot make these readily available. Thus, universal and generous welfare systems ensure that – to varying degrees – these technologies are experienced more widely. Where these systems, particularly health systems, are not universal in nature and are heavily means tested, this lessens the likelihood that the benefits of this technology are evenly distributed. Thus, the US spends the largest amount of money on the planet on healthcare, yet access to healthcare is largely dictated by income – as we saw in Chapter Four, the US has one of the highest rates of infant mortality among advanced industrial nations.

Fettering capital

Societies that place greater *fetters on the extraction of surplus value* tend to produce less exploitative and, therefore, less injurious modes of production. The impulses of capitalist logic to continually 'sweat' the labour relation to extract greater levels of surplus value, left unrestrained, provide the generative contexts that explain the variance in capitalist harms. Indeed, the greater the fetters that are placed on the ability to extract 'more for less' from workers by lengthening the working day or exerting downward pressure on wages, or restricting the extension of the logic of cost benefit analyses that incorporate human safety into this 'amoral' calculus, the less harmful these relations become. Thus, those societies that are willing to intervene and to organise aspects of the workplace, and more broadly, the operation of markets, appear to lessen the harmful impacts of capitalist relations.

Fetters appear to come in two principal forms. First, trade union representation in the workplace produces more humane working conditions – the analyses presented in Chapter Five demonstrate this relationship in relation to a range of autonomy harms. The impact of worker representation has a direct impact in relation to long working hours, so that those nation states that have longer working days tend to have low rates of worker representation. The impact of unionism appears to be broader; for example, with harms such as poverty, higher rates of union membership appear to reduce these harms, in all likelihood because of the impact of collective bargaining on wages, and therefore reducing the extent of 'in-work' poverty. Without available comparative workplace death and injury figures, the study is unable to comment on the impact of trade unions in this regard; nevertheless, the available studies suggest that unionised workplaces prove to be safer, as worker representation foregrounds safety concerns within business decisions, countering the commodification of human lives (Slapper and Tombs, 1998). Second, state intervention through regulatory law and agencies can also have the effect of fettering the exploitative function of capital. Unfortunately, it is difficult to assess the impact of state regulatory systems and the fetters it places on the processes of surplus value with little comparative data available in relation to regulatory activities. It is interesting to note, however, the harm reduction function of state regulatory activities in relation to the autonomy harms outlined in Chapter Five, more specifically, the role of regulations that limit the length of the working day, or the impact of redundancy regulations that serve to militate against the harms for young people resulting from the loss of a job.

It is difficult to succinctly summarise the features that reduce harm – they are varied and interrelate in complex ways – but if compelled to, a recurring theme of the analyses throughout the book is 'social organisation'. Societies that organise themselves into solidaristic forms choose to regulate workplaces, markets and fetter individual freedoms, and create universal and generous welfare states are less harmful capitalist forms. Yet these features are the antithesis of the neoliberal regime, characterised by deregulated markets, residual welfare systems and highly individualised and fragmented societies. As neoliberalism has embedded within the varieties of capitalist formation, it has brought a series of 'disorganising' logics that have sought to dismantle and erode many aspects of harm reduction in these 'host' societies in order to promote 'free markets' and 'individual freedoms'. The impact of neoliberalism is not tracked across time in this study; nevertheless, it is fair to suggest, from the data analysed, that significant variance remains among capitalist form in terms of harm reduction. Thus, neoliberalism has had an uneven impact across the different regimes presented, with in particular the social democratic, and to a lesser degree, the northern corporatist regimes demonstrating the greatest forms of resistance to the 'restructuring ethos' of neoliberalism in terms of harm reduction – as existing cultures and structures appear to be more resilient to this ethos.

If neoliberalism had appeared to lose its intellectual verve during the 2000s and credibility in the immediate aftermath of the credit crunch, it has proved to be 'resurgent' in the guise of the 'austerity' programmes rolled out across the Eurozone and the UK. Those nation states that had been forced to provide 'life support' for their ailing banks were now heavily indebted, and consequently engaged in fierce austerity programmes, the implication being that neoliberalism – which arguably lay at the heart of the credit crunch – in various guises, was becoming further embedded into host systems and its 'disorganising logics' reinvigorated by the aftermath of the crisis. Most troubling, on the basis of this analysis, is that it is those facets of societies that serve to reduce harms that are being dismantled – in particular, social expenditure. It is difficult to capture at this point the collateral damage of the austerity programmes, as an insufficient time lag has taken place in order to be able to collect data that can discern patterns in the incidence of harms. Nevertheless, as we know, the housing repossessions that took place in the wake of the Spanish financial crisis led to a peak in Spanish suicide rates (Lopez Bernal et al, 2013). The point is that as austerity unfolds, in countries like Greece, Spain,

Portugal and the UK, nation states that have engaged in devastating austerity programmes will witness significant rises in specific harms.

Resurgent neoliberalism, enduring capitalism.... What does the social harm perspective offer?

This does not seem to be a very optimistic point to conclude the book. In fact, it is difficult to be optimistic in the wake of the latest capitalist crisis and the devastating social wreckage that has resulted, particularly as capitalism's enduring resilience remains unshaken, and is, in many nation states, flourishing, in the guise of resurgent neoliberalism, as the archetypal 'crisis theory'. As the 'crisis theory' found its latest expression within the politics of austerity, neoliberalism has sought to further retrench the 'social' state and remove further 'impediments' to wealth accumulation, and has done little to address the structural failings within finance capital that led to the credit crunch. Many advanced industrialised economies are faced, then, with rising inequalities, stagnating wages and falling living standards, combined with the spectre of further economic instability and the contagion of the Eurozone; neoliberalism has unleashed a series of harmful social forces that threatens to further destabilise capitalism. Put bluntly, repeated crises are more difficult to explain. Indeed, utilitarian notions that capitalist harm should be tolerated in exchange for the benefits that this mode of organisation brings become more untenable if further crises unfold. While neoliberalism appears to have stolen a march in the aftermath of the credit crunch, the 'patch' it has placed onto the current configuration of capitalism further imbues our societies with volatility, and in doing so, it has shaped a future terrain that the social harm perspective is well placed to illuminate.

The assertion that the social harm approach is well situated to articulate challenges to the production of capitalist harm in the post-recession conjuncture requires further interrogation and elaboration. In fact, Garside (2013) has argued that making neoliberalism the focus of social harm analyses to date has restricted the emancipatory potential of the critique. He continues to argue that a dominant characteristic feature of the social harm approach is 'a prior acceptance of the capitalist order as the only possible mode of social organisation' (2013, p 252). Ultimately, for Garside (2013), these works contribute more to the better regulation of capitalism than the transformation of capitalist relations into alternate forms. Garside (2013) is certainly correct that thus far a significant proportion of the analytical attention of social harm analysis has fallen onto the harmful impacts of neoliberalism in its various guises. Even though much of the analysis presented here grounds harm production within capitalist relations, the analytical attention afforded to 'more or less harmful' capitalisms does little to placate Garside's concerns.

It goes without saying that the reformist versus transformative critique dilemma is not unique to the social harm approach – numerous critical approaches have engaged with the tension between immediate and albeit short-lived alleviation of specific harms and the possibility of more permanent structural change. These tensions are probably irreconcilable; there is no easy and obvious way to 'square the circle', and neither can an individual work begin to suggest a way out of this labyrinth. It is certainly accepted here that by engaging in the 'here and now' to articulate a more humane and less injurious capitalist form, that these very engagements may contribute to hegemonies that sustain and secure rather than destabilise capitalist relations. Whether or not shifting capitalism into a more humane and less injurious form would open out a political terrain, where the possibility for alternative social forms are more likely to take hold, is speculation. Yet this is a persuasive position (and perhaps the only position available) given the political realities and constraints in which we currently operate, combined with the necessity to halt and reverse the 'restructuring' logics of neoliberalism. In short, analyses of 'more or less' harmful societies provide a necessary starting position, rather than the end point and the sum of our collective ambition.

Perhaps one of the most important arguments that the social harm perspective can make in relation to social transformation is the idea that harms are ultimately preventable insofar as they are grounded in alterable social relations. Gaining acceptance for the notion that societies 'design in' and 'design out' harms from the fabric of social relations is critical to alternative social forms taking hold. This is not restricted to the diagnosis of 'more and less' harmful capitalist forms, and the move of existing structures from the former to the latter, but if the argument is accepted, that the transformation of specific capitalist forms is possible, then it is entirely plausible that these questions may be posed of capitalist relations more broadly. In other words 'more or less' harmful capitalist forms becomes a narrative device through which we can convincingly articulate the point that harms result from 'alterable', rather than immutable, social relations. Ultimately, the 'harms' we are willing to tolerate become a moral and philosophical question, rather than a question of what is practically possible.

Naturally, if we merely restrict such visions to less harmful forms of capitalism, our ability to provide alternatives that are likely to transform social relations will be seriously circumscribed, as Garside (2013) suggests. However, it is also entirely possible that analyses of the 'here and now' begin to open out concrete strategies for social transformation behind which social forces might augment. An obvious starting place for such discussions would be the characteristics of contemporary societies – as discussed in the previous section – that serve to ameliorate harms, and from which we might begin to glean ways of not just better regulating capitalism, but also understanding alternative, less harmful modes of social organisation. If we take Clarke's (2004) notion of the 'public', this encapsulates many of the features of societies that inhibit the production of capitalist harm – particularly social solidarity and decommodification, discussed earlier. For Clarke (2004), the 'public' provides the 'grit' that currently obstructs the disorganising logics of neoliberalism. The 'public', as Clarke explains, refers 'to a number of intersecting social phenomena: the idea of a public interest which may require forms of collectivised expression; the institutionalisation of "public services" (as a means of meeting the public's needs); and the conception of a public – a collective (usually national) body that is capable of having interests and needs' (2004, p 27). Indeed, by identifying the 'grit' and by considering ways that this might further be expanded to not only roll back 'neoliberalism' but also to consider ways that we might, in turn, transcend capitalist relations, offers long-term transformative potential. Indeed, it is not difficult to imagine how the boundaries of the 'public' might be rearticulated and expanded to consider alternative means of ownership through a 'public commons', as well as more democratic forms of production and distribution that are principally organised to meet human needs. The 'public' offers an opportunity to move from the starting position located within the current conjuncture, to apply the brakes to 'the runaway train' that is neoliberalism, and to begin to orientate the design of our societies to resemble something closer to what we might imagine the 'harm free' society to look like.

Harmful societies has raised numerous complex issues in relation to the social harm approach, namely, how we define harm; how we measure harm; and how we prevent harm. It does not purport to offer a prescriptive guide or ready-made solutions to these questions. Rather, its intention from the outset has been to demonstrate the form that a social harm lens might take, and the ways in which this lens may be applied to begin to understand the complex mass of harm production in capitalist societies. Through documenting the variance of harms between differing capitalist forms, it has sought to challenge the notion that social harms are unavoidable 'accidents', 'facts of life', or 'quirks of fate'; rather, as we have seen, the forms that capitalist societies take have a significant impact on rates of harm. Those capitalist societies that are the least harmful are those that cling most dearly to the various constituent parts of the 'social state' in the face of the restructuring logics of neoliberalism. In an era of austerity, it is these very harm reduction structures that are under attack. It is imperative that the social harm approach articulates the defence and expansion of these structures; otherwise the collateral harms that result will be grave, a legacy that will extend well beyond the current generation.

References

Amagasa, T., Nakayama, T. and Takahashi, Y. (2005) 'Karojisatsu in Japan: characteristics of 22 cases of work-related suicide', *Journal of Occupational Health*, vol 47, no 2, pp 157-64.

Ameratunga, S., Hijar, M. and Norton, R. (2006) 'Road-traffic injuries: confronting disparities to address a global-health problem', *The Lancet*, vol 367, no 9521, pp 1533-40.

Anxo, D. (2009) 'Working time policy in Sweden', in JILPT (Japan Institute for Labour Policy and Training), *Working time – In search of new research territories beyond flexibility debates*, 2009 JILPT Workshop on Working Time, Tokyo: JILPT, pp 55-70.

Arntzen, A. and Andersen, A.M.N. (2004) 'Social determinants for infant mortality in the Nordic countries, 1980-2001', *Scandinavian Journal of Public Health*, vol 32, no 5, pp 381-9.

Artazcoz, L., Cortès, I., Escribà-Agüir, V., Cascant, L. and Villegas, R. (2009) 'Understanding the relationship of long working hours with health status and health-related behaviours', *Journal of Epidemiology and Community Health*, vol 63, no 7, pp 521-7.

Arts, W. and Gelissen, J. (2002) 'Three worlds of welfare capitalism or more? A state-of-the-art report', *Journal of European Social Policy*, vol 12, no 2, pp 137-58.

Arulampalam, W. (2001) 'Is unemployment really scarring? Effects of unemployment experiences on wages', *The Economic Journal*, vol 111, no 475, pp 585-606.

Baker, D. and Taylor, H. (1997) 'The relationship between condition-specific morbidity, social support and material deprivation in pregnancy and early motherhood. ALSPAC Survey Team. Avon Longitudinal Study of Pregnancy and Childhood', *Social Science & Medicine*, vol 45, no 9, pp 1073-83.

Ballesteros, M.F., Dischinger, P.C. and Langenberg, P. (2004) 'Pedestrian injuries and vehicle type in Maryland, 1995-1999', *Accident Analysis & Prevention*, vol 36, no 1, pp 73-81.

Batty, E. and Flint, J. (2010) *Self-esteem, comparative poverty and neighbourhoods*, York: Joseph Rowntree Foundation.

Beckett, K. and Western, B. (2001) 'Governing social marginality: welfare, incarceration, and the transformation of state policy', *Punishment & Society*, vol 3, no 1, pp 43-59.

Bell, D.N.F. and Blanchflower, D.G. (2011) *Young people and the Great Recession*, Discussion Paper No 5674, Bonn: Institute for the Study of Labor (IZA).

Berg, P., Appelbaum, E., Bailey, T. and Kalleberg, A.L. (2004) 'Contesting time: international comparisons of employee control of working time', *Industrial & Labour Relations Review*, vol 57, no 3, April.

Blau, J. and Blau, P. (1982) 'The cost of inequality: metropolitan structure and violent crime', *American Sociological Review*, vol 47, pp 114-28.

Blumstein, A. and Wallman, J. (2005) 'The recent rise and fall of American violence', in A. Blumstein and J. Wallman (eds) *The crime drop in America*, Cambridge: Cambridge University Press, pp 1-12.

Boyer, R. (2005) *How and why capitalisms differ*, Cologne: Max Planck Institute for the Study of Societies.

Bradley, R.H. and Corwyn, R.F. (2002) 'Socioeconomic status and child development', *Annual Review of Psychology*, vol 53, no 1, pp 371-99.

Bradshaw, J. (2002) 'Child poverty and child outcomes', *Children & Society*, vol 16, no 2, pp 131-40.

Bradshaw, J. (2006) *A review of the comparative evidence on child poverty*, York: Joseph Rowntree Foundation.

Bruff, I. (2011) 'What about the elephant in the room? Varieties of capitalism, varieties in capitalism', *New Political Economy*, vol 16, no 4, pp 481-500.

Cain, M. and Howe, A. (eds) (2008) *Women, crime and social harm: Towards a criminology for the global era*, Oxford: Hart.

Callinicos, A. (2001) *Against the third way: An anti-capitalist critique*, Cambridge: Polity Press.

Callinicos, A. (2006) *The resources of critique*, Cambridge: Polity Press.

Caminada, K., Goudswaard, K. and Koster, F. (2012) 'Social income transfers and poverty: a cross-country analysis for OECD countries', *International Journal of Social Welfare*, vol 21, no 2, pp 115-26.

Card, D., Lemieux, T. and Craig Riddel, W. (2003) *Unionization and wage inequality: A comparative study of the US, the UK and Canada*, NBER Working Paper 9473, Cambridge, MA: National Bureau of Economic Research.

Carter, P. (2003) *Managing offenders, reducing crime: A new approach*, London: Cabinet Office Strategy Unit.

Cavadino, M. and Dignan, J. (2006) 'Penal policy and political economy', *Criminology and Criminal Justice*, vol 6, no 4, pp 435-56.

Cerny, P., Menz, G. and Soederberg, S. (2005) 'Introduction: Different roads to globalization: Neoliberalism, the competition state, and politics in a more open world', in S. Soederberg, G. Menz and P. Cerny (eds) *Internalizing globalization: The rise and the decline of national varieties of capitalism*, Basingstoke: Palgrave Macmillan.

Chandran, A., Hyder, A.A. and Peek-Asa, C. (2010) 'The global burden of unintentional injuries and an agenda for progress', *Epidemiologic Reviews*, vol 32, no 1, pp 110-20.

Chang, S.-S., Gunnell, D., Sterne, J.A., Lu, T.-H. and Cheng, A.T. (2009) 'Was the economic crisis 1997-1998 responsible for rising suicide rates in East/Southeast Asia? A time–trend analysis for Japan, Hong Kong, South Korea, Taiwan, Singapore and Thailand', *Social Science & Medicine*, vol 68, no 7, pp 1322-31.

Christie, N., Cairns, S., Towner, E. and Ward, H. (2007) 'How exposure information can enhance our understanding of child traffic "death leagues"', *Injury Prevention*, vol 13, no 2, pp 125-9.

Chung, H. and Muntaner, C. (2006) 'Political and welfare state determinants of infant and child health indicators: an analysis of wealthy countries', *Social Science & Medicine*, vol 63, no 3, pp 829-84.

Clarke, J. (2004) 'Dissolving the public realm? The logics and limits of neo-liberalism', *Journal of Social Policy*, vol 33, no 1, pp 27-48.

Coburn, D. (2004) 'Beyond the income inequality hypothesis: class, neo-liberalism, and health inequalities', *Social Science & Medicine*, vol 58, no 1, pp 41-56.

Cohen, R., Coxall, J., Craig, G. and Sadiq-Sangster, A. (1992) *Hardship Britain: Being poor in the 1990s*, London: Child Poverty Action Group.

Cohen, S. (1993) 'Human rights and crimes of the state: the culture of denial', *Australian and New Zealand Journal of Criminology*, vol 26, no 2, pp 97-115.

Coleman, R., Sim, J., Tombs, S. and Whyte, D. (2009) 'Introduction: State, power, crime', in R. Coleman, J. Sim, S. Tombs and D. Whyte (eds) *State, power, crime*, London: Sage.

COMEAP (Committee on Medial Effects of Air Pollution) (2010) *The mortality effects of long term exposure to particulate air pollution in the United Kingdom*, London: Health Protection Agency.

Conley, D. and Springer, K.W. (2001) 'Welfare state and infant mortality', *American Journal of Sociology*, vol 107, no 3, pp 768-807.

Crouch, C. and Streeck, W. (1997) *Political economy of modern capitalism: Mapping convergence and diversity*, London: Sage.

Deacon, B. (2007) *Global social policy and governance*, London: Sage.

Deeg, R. and Jackson, G. (2007) 'Towards a more dynamic theory of capitalist variety', *Socio-Economic Review*, vol 5, pp 149-79.

Dickens, A.P., Richards, S.H., Greaves, C.J. and Campbell, J.L. (2011) 'Interventions targeting social isolation in older people: a systematic review', *BMC Public Health*, vol 11, no 1, pp 647-69.

Doody, J. (2010) 'Exclusion orders under the Prevention of Terrorism Acts 1974-1989: A social harm analysis', PhD, Coleraine: University of Ulster.

Dorling, D. (2004) 'Prime suspect: murder in Britain', in P. Hillyard, C. Pantazis, S. Tombs and D. Gordon (eds) *Beyond criminology: Taking harm seriously*, London: Pluto Press, Chapter 11.

Dorling, D., Gordon, D., Hillyard, P., Pantazis, C., Pemberton, S. and Tombs, S. (2008) *Criminal obsessions: Why harm matters more than crime*, London: Centre for Crime and Justice Studies.

Doyal, L. and Gough, I. (1984) 'A theory of human needs', *Critical Social Policy*, vol 4, no 10, pp 6-38.

Doyal, L. and Gough, I. (1991) *A theory of human need*, Basingstoke: Palgrave Macmillan.

Dumenil, G. and Levy, D. (2004) *Capital resurgent: Roots of the neoliberal revolution*, Cambridge, MA: Harvard University Press.

Duncan, G.J., Yeung, W.J., Brooks-Gunn, J. and Smith, J.R. (1998) 'How much does childhood poverty affect the life chances of children?', *American Sociological Review*, pp 406-23.

Eckersley, R. and Dear, K. (2002) 'Cultural correlates of youth suicide', *Social Science & Medicine*, vol 55, no 11, pp 1891-904.

Engels, F. (1845/1987) *The condition of the working class in England*, London: Penguin.

Esping-Andersen, G. (1990) *The three worlds of welfare capitalism*, Cambridge: Polity Press.

Esping-Andersen, G. (1999) *Social foundations of post-industrial economies*, Oxford: Oxford University Press.

Esping-Andersen, G. and Wagner, S. (2012) 'Asymmetries in the opportunity structure. Intergenerational mobility trends in Europe', *Research in Social Stratification and Mobility*, vol 30, no 4, pp 473-87.

Ezeonu, I. (2008) 'Crimes of globalisation: health care, HIV and the poverty of neo-liberalism in sub-Saharan Africa', *International Journal of Social Inquiry*, vol 1, no 2, pp 113-34.

Fagnani, J. and Letablier, M.-T. (2004) 'Work and family life balance: the impact of the 35-hour laws in France', *Work, Employment & Society*, vol 18, no 3, pp 551-72.

Fahmy, E. and Pemberton, S. (2012) 'A video testimony on rural poverty and social exclusion', *Sociological Research Online*, vol 17, no 1, p 2.

Faust, K. and Kauzlarich, D. (2008) 'Hurricane Katrina victimization as a state crime of omission', *Critical Criminology*, vol 16, no 2, pp 85-103.

Ferguson, I., Lavalette, M. and Mooney, G. (2002) *Rethinking welfare: A critical perspective*, London: Sage.

Ferrie, J.E., Shipley, M.J., Stansfeld, S.A., Davey Smith, G. and Marmot, M. (2003) 'Future uncertainty and socioeconomic inequalities in health: the Whitehall II Study', *Social Science & Medicine*, vol 57, no 4, pp 637-46.

Findlay, R. (2003) 'Interventions to reduce social isolation amongst older people: where is the evidence?', *Ageing & Society*, vol 23, no 5, pp 647-58.

Flint, J. (2010) *Coping strategies? Agencies, budgeting and self-esteem amongst low-income households*, York: Joseph Rowntree Foundation.

Foucault, M. and Chomsky, N. (1997) 'Human nature: justice versus power', in A. Davidson (ed) *Foucault and his interlocutors*, London: The University of Chicago Press, pp 107-45.

Fraser, D. (2009) *The evolution of the British welfare state: A history of social policy since the Industrial Revolution*, Basingstoke: Palgrave Macmillan.

Friel, S., Chopra, M. and Satcher, D. (2007) 'Unequal weight: equity-oriented policy responses to the global obesity epidemic', *British Medical Journal*, vol 335, no 7632, pp 1241-3.

Gamble, A. (1988) *The free economy and the strong state: The politics of Thatcherism*, London: Macmillan.

Gamble, A. (2009) *The spectre at the feast: Capitalist crisis and the politics of recession*, Basingstoke: Palgrave Macmillan.

Garside, R. (2013) 'Addressing social harm: better regulation versus social transformation', *Revisita Critica Penal y Poder*, vol 5, pp 247-65.

Geras, N. (1985) 'The controversy about Marx and justice', *New Left Review*, vol 150 (March-April), pp 47-85.

Gill, S. (2003) *Power and resistance in the new world order*, Basingstoke: Palgrave Macmillan.

Gordon, D. (2004) 'Poverty, death and disease', in P. Hillyard, C. Pantazis, S. Tombs and D. Gordon (eds) *Beyond criminology: Taking harm seriously*, London: Pluto Press, Chapter 15.

Gordon, D. and Pantazis, C. (1997) *Breadline Britain in the 1990s*, Aldershot: Ashgate Publishing.

Gough, I. (1979) *The political economy of the welfare state*, London: Macmillan.

Gramsci, A. (1971) *Selections from the prison notebooks of Antonio Gramsci*, New York: International Publishers.

Greenfield, V. and Paoli, L. (2013) 'A framework to assess the harms of crimes', *British Journal of Criminology*, vol 53, no 5, pp 864-85.

Gregg, P. (2001) 'The impact of youth unemployment on adult unemployment in the NCDS', *The Economic Journal*, vol 111, no 475, pp 626-53.

Gregg, P. and Tominey, E. (2005) 'The wage scar from male youth unemployment', *Labour Economics*, vol 12, no 4, pp 487-509.

Hall, P. and Soskice, D. (2001) *Varieties of capitalism: The institutional foundations of comparative advantage*, Oxford: Oxford University Press.

Hancke, B., Rhodes, M. and Thatcher, M. (2007) *Beyond varieties of capitalism: Conflict, contradictions and complementarities in the European economy*, Oxford: Oxford University Press.

Harrington, J.M. (2001) 'Health effects of shift work and extended hours of work', *Occupational and Environmental Medicine*, vol 58, no 1, pp 68-72.

Harvey, D. (2007a) *A brief history of neoliberalism*, Oxford: Oxford University Press.

Harvey, D. (2007b) *The limits to capital*, London: Verso.

Harvey, D. (2010) *The enigma of capital and the crises of capitalism*, London: Profile Books.

Hawkes, C. (2006) 'Uneven dietary development: linking the policies and processes of globalization with the nutrition transition, obesity and diet-related chronic diseases', *Globalization and Health*, vol 2, no 1, pp 4-22.

Hay, C. (2004) 'The normalising role of rationalist assumptions in the institutional embedding of neoliberalism', *Economy & Society*, vol 33, no 4, pp 500-27.

Hayek, F. (1944/76) *The road to serfdom*, London: Routledge & Kegan Paul.

Helliwell, J.F. (2007) 'Well-being and social capital: does suicide pose a puzzle?', *Social Indicators Research*, vol 81, no 3, pp 455-96.

Hillyard, P. and Tombs, S. (2004) 'Beyond criminology?', in P. Hillyard, C. Pantazis, S. Tombs and D. Gordon (eds) *Beyond criminology: Taking harm seriously*, London: Pluto Press, Chapter 2.

Hillyard, P., Pantazis, C., Tombs, S. and Gordon, D. (eds) (2004) *Beyond criminology: Taking harm seriously*, London: Pluto Press.

Holt-Lunstad, J., Smith, T.B. and Layton, J.B. (2010) 'Social relationships and mortality risk: a meta-analytic review', *PLOS Medicine*, vol 7, no 7, e1000316.

Hope, A. (2013) 'The shackled school internet: zemiological solutions to the problem of over-blocking', *Learning, Media and Technology*, vol 38, no 3, pp 270-83.

House, J.S., Landis, K.R. and Umberson, D. (1988) 'Social relationships and health', *Science*, vol 241, no 4865, pp 540-5.

HSE (Health and Safety Executive) (2014) *Health and safety statistics for Great Britain 2013/2014*, http://www.hse.gov.uk.ezproxye.bham.ac.uk/statistics/overall/hssh1314.pdf

Hughes, G. (2006) 'Book review: *Beyond criminology: Taking harm seriously*', *Social & Legal Studies*, vol 15, no 1, pp 157-9.

Hutton, W. (1995) *The state we're in*, London: Jonathan Cape.

Jacobs, D. and Richardson, A. (2008) 'Economic inequality and homicide in the developed nations from 1975 to 1995', *Homicide Studies*, vol 12, no 1, pp 28-45.

Jacobs, G., Thomas, A.A. and Astrop, A. (2000) *Estimating global road fatalities*, Crowthorne: Transport Research Laboratory.

Jäntti, M., Bratsberg, B., Røed, K., Raaum, O., Naylor, R., Österbacka, E., Oddbjørn, B. and Eriksson, T. (2006) *American exceptionalism in a new light – A comparison of intergenerational earnings mobility in the Nordic countries, the United Kingdom and the United States*, Discussion Paper 1938, Berlin: Institute for the Study of Labor (IZA).

Johnson, G., Krug, E. and Potter, L. (2000) 'Suicide among adolescents and young adults: a cross-national comparison of 34 countries', *Suicide and Life-Threatening Behavior*, vol 30, no 1, pp 74-82.

Kim, D.M., Ahn, C.W. and Nam, S.Y. (2005) 'Prevalence of obesity in Korea', *Obesity Reviews*, vol 6, no 2, pp 117-21.

Klein, N. (2007) *The shock doctrine: The rise of disaster capitalism*, London: Penguin/Allen Lane.

Kleppa, E., Sanne, B. and Tell, G.S. (2008) 'Working overtime is associated with anxiety and depression: the Hordaland Health Study', *Journal of Occupational and Environmental Medicine*, vol 50, no 6, pp 658-66.

Kramer, R. (1985) 'Defining the concept of crime: a humanistic perspective', *Journal of Sociology and Social Welfare*, vol 12, no 3, pp 469-87.

Langley, J. (2001) 'International comparisons: we need to know a lot more', *Injury Prevention*, vol 7, no 4, pp 267-9.

Lasslett, K. (2010) 'Crime or social harm? A dialectical perspective', *Crime, Law and Social Change*, vol 54, no 1, pp 1-19.

Lederman, D., Loayza, N. and Menéndez, A. (2002) 'Violent crime: does social capital matter?', *Economic Development and Cultural Change*, vol 50, no 3, pp 509-39.

Lister, R. (2003) *Poverty*, Cambridge: Polity Press.

Lopez Bernal, J.A., Gasparrini, A. and Artundo, C.M. (2013) 'The effect of the late 2000s financial crisis on suicides in Spain: an interrupted time-series analysis', *European Journal of Public Health*, vol 23, no 5, pp 732-6.

Lynch, J., Kaplan, G. and Shema, S. (1997) 'Cumulative impact of sustained economic hardship on physical cognitive, psychological and social functioning', *New England Journal of Medicine*, vol 337, pp 1889-5.

McGuire, M. (2007) *Hypercrime: The new geometry of harm*, Abingdon: Routledge Cavendish.

Marmot, M. (2005) 'Social determinants of health inequalities', *The Lancet*, vol 365, no 9464, pp 1099-104.

Marx, K. (1844/1963) *Karl Marx on sociology and social philosophy*, Harmondsworth: Penguin.

Messner, S. and Rosenfeld, R. (1997) 'Political restraint of the market and levels of criminal homicide: a cross-national application of institutional anomie theory', *Social Forces*, vol 75, no 4, pp 1393-416.

Michalowski, R. (1985) *Order, law and crime*, New York: Random House.

Michalowski, R. (2011) 'In search of "state and crime" in state crime studies', in W.J. Chambliss, R. Michalowski and R. Kramer (eds) *State crime in the global age*, Cullompton: Willan Publishing, Chapter 2.

Milner, A., McClure, R. and Diego, D. (2012) 'Socio-economic determinants of suicide: an ecological analysis of 35 countries', *Social Psychiatry and Psychiatric Epidemiology*, vol 47, no 1, pp 19-27.

Mroz, T.A. and Savage, T.H. (2006) 'The long-term effects of youth unemployment', *Journal of Human Resources*, vol 41, no 2, pp 259-93.

Muncie, J. (2000) 'Decriminalising criminology', in G. Lewis, S. Gerwitz and J. Clarke (eds) *Rethinking social policy*, London: Sage, pp 217-28.

Muncie, J. (2005) 'Book review: *Beyond criminology: Taking harm seriously*', *Crime, Law and Social Change*, vol 43, no 2, pp 199-201.

Muschamp, Y., Bullock, K., Ridge, T. and Wikeley, F. (2009) '"Nothing to do": the impact of poverty on pupils' learning identities within out-of-school activities', *British Educational Research Journal*, vol 35, no 2, pp 305-21.

Naughton, M. (2007) *Re-thinking miscarriages of justice: Beyond the tip of the iceberg*, London: Palgrave Macmillan.

Nesvetailova, A. (2005) 'Globalization and post-Soviet capitalism: internalizing neoliberalism in Russia', in S. Soederberg, G. Menz and P. Cerny (eds) *Internalizing globalization: The rise and the decline of national varieties of capitalism*, Basingstoke: Palgrave Macmillan, pp 238-54.

Novak, T. (1988) *Poverty and the state: An historical sociology*, Milton Keynes: Open University Press.

Obermeyr, Z., Murray, C. and Gakidou, E. (2008) 'Fifty years of violent war deaths from Vietnam to Bosnia: analysis of data from the world health survey programme', *British Medical Journal*, vol 336, no 7659, pp 1482-86.

O'Connor, J. (2010) 'Marxism and the three movements of neoliberalism', *Critical Sociology*, vol 36, no 5, pp 691-715.

OECD (Organisation for Economic Co-operation and Development) (2011) 'Suicide', in *Health at a Glance 2011*, OECD Indicators, Paris: OECD Publishing.

Office for National Statistics (2014) Excess Winter Mortality in England and Wales, 2013/14 (Provisional) and 2012/2013 (Final), Newport: ONS.

Önis, Z. and Güven, A. (2011) 'The global economic crisis and the future of neoliberal globalization: rupture versus continuity', *Global Governance*, vol 17, no 4, pp 469-88.

Ouimet, M. (2012) 'A world of homicides: the effect of economic development, income inequality, and excess infant mortality on the homicide rate for the 165 countries in 2010', *Homicide Studies*, vol 16, no 3, pp 238-58.

Page, D. (2000) *Communities in the balance: The reality of social exclusion on housing estates*, York: Joseph Rowntree Foundation.

Pantazis, C. (2004) 'Gendering harm through a life course perspective', in P. Hillyard, C. Pantazis, S. Tombs and D. Gordon (eds) *Beyond criminology: Taking harm seriously*, London: Pluto Press, Chapter 12.

Pantazis, C. and Pemberton, S. (2009) 'Nation states and the production of social harm: resisting the hegemony of "TINA"', in R. Coleman, J. Sim, S. Tombs and D. Whyte (eds) *State, power, crime*, London: Sage, pp 214-23.

Payne, S. (2006) 'Mental health, poverty and social exclusion', in C. Pantazis, D. Gordon and R. Levitas (eds) *Poverty and social exclusion in Britain: The Millennium Survey*, Bristol: Policy Press, pp 285-314.

Peck, J., Theodore, N. and Brenner, N. (2010) 'Post-neoliberalism and its malcontents', *Antipode*, vol 41, no 1, pp 94-116.

Pemberton, S. (2004a) 'The production of harm in the United Kingdom: A social harm perspective', PhD, Bristol: University of Bristol.

Pemberton, S. (2004b) 'A theory of moral indifference: understanding the production of harm by capitalist society', in P. Hillyard, C. Pantazis, S. Tombs and D. Gordon (eds) *Beyond criminology: Taking harm seriously*, London: Pluto Press, Chapter 5.

Pemberton, S. (2007) 'Social harm future(s): exploring the potential of the social harm approach', *Crime, Law and Social Change*, vol 48, no 1, pp 27-41.

Pickett, K.E., Kelly, S., Brunner, E., Lobstein, T. and Wilkinson, R.G. (2005) 'Wider income gaps, wider waistbands? An ecological study of obesity and income inequality', *Journal of Epidemiology and Community Health*, vol 59, no 8, pp 670-4.

Plant, R. (1998) 'Citizenship, rights, welfare', in J. Franklin (ed) *Social policy and social justice*, London: Institute for Public Policy Research, pp 57-72.

Poulantzas, N. (1978) *State, power, socialism*, London: Verso.

Presser, L. (2013) *Why we harm*, New Brunswick, NJ: Rutgers University Press.

Pridemore, W. (2010) 'Poverty matters: a reassessment of the inequality-homicide relationship in cross-national studies', *British Journal of Criminology*, vol 51, pp 739-72.

Pucher, J. and Buehler, R. (2008) 'Making cycling irresistible: lessons from the Netherlands, Denmark and Germany', *Transport Reviews*, vol 28, no 4, pp 495-528.

Rosenheck, R. (2008) 'Fast food consumption and increased caloric intake: a systematic review of a trajectory towards weight gain and obesity risk', *Obesity Reviews*, vol 9, no 6, pp 535-47.

Saunders, P., Sutherland, K., Davidson, P., Hampshire, A., King, S. and Taylor, J. (2006) *Experiencing poverty: The voices of low-income Australians: Towards new indicators of disadvantage project. Stage 1: focus group outcomes*. Sydney: Social Policy Research Centre.

Savolainen, J. (2000) 'Inequality, welfare state, and homicide: further support for the institutional anomie theory', *Criminology*, vol 38, no 4, pp 1021-42.

Scarpetta, S., Sonnet, A. and Manfredi, T. (2010) *Rising youth unemployment during the crisis: How to prevent negative long-term consequences on a generation*, OECD Social, Employment and Migration Working Papers, No 106, Paris: OECD Publishing.

Schroeder, M. (2009) 'Integrating welfare and production typologies: how refinements of the varieties of capitalism approach call for a combination of welfare typologies', *Journal of Social Policy*, vol 38, no 1, pp 19-43.

Schwendinger, H. and Schwendinger, J. (1970) 'Defenders of order or guardians of human rights', *Issues in Criminology*, vol 5, no 2, pp 123-57.

Schwendinger, H. and Schwendinger, J. (1975) 'Defenders of order or guardians of human rights', in I. Taylor, P. Walton and J. Young (eds), *Critical criminology*, London: Routledge and Kegan Paul, pp 113-46.

Schwendinger, H. and Schwendingder, J. (2001) 'Defenders of order or guardians of human rights?', in S. Henry and M.M. Lanier (eds) *What is crime? Controversies over the nature of crime and what to do about it*, Lanham, MD: Rowman & Littlefield Publishers, Chapter 7.

Scruggs, L. and Allan, J.P. (2006) 'The material consequences of welfare states: benefit generosity and absolute poverty in 16 OECD countries', *Comparative Political Studies*, vol 39, no 7, pp 880-904.

Shields, M. (1999) 'Long working hours and health', *Health Reports-Statistics Canada*, vol 11, pp 33-48.

Slapper, G. and Tombs, S. (1999) *Corporate crime*, London: Longman.

Smith, D.M. (2005) *On the margins of inclusion: Changing labour markets and social exclusion in London*, Bristol: Policy Press.

Soederberg, S. (2005) 'The rise of neoliberalism in Mexico: From developmental to competition state', in S. Soederberg, G. Menz and P. Cerny (eds) *Internalizing globalization: The rise and the decline of national varieties of capitalism*, Basingstoke: Palgrave Macmillan, pp 167-82.

Soper, K. (1981) *On human needs*, Brighton: Harvester.

Spelman, W. (2005) 'The limited importance of prison expansion', in A. Blumstein and J. Wallman (eds) *The crime drop in America*, Cambridge: Cambridge University Press, pp 97-129.

Stuckler, D., Basu, S., Suhrcke, M., Coutts, A. and McKee, M. (2009) 'The public health effect of economic crises and alternative policy responses in Europe: an empirical analysis', *The Lancet*, vol 374, no 9686, pp 315-23.

Supiot, A. (2013) 'Grandeur and misery of the social state', *New Left Review*, vol 82 (July/August), pp 99-113.

Sutherland, E.H. (1940) 'White-collar criminality', *American Sociological Review*, vol 5, no 1, pp 1-12.

Sutherland, E.H. (1945) 'Is "white-collar crime" crime?', *American Sociological Review*, vol 10, no 2, pp 132-9.

Sutton, L., Smith, N., Dearden, C. and Middleton, S. (2007) *A child's eye view of social difference*, York: Joseph Rowntree Foundation.

Tan, G. (2011) 'Structuration theory and wrongful imprisonment: from "victimhood" to "survivorship"?', *Critical Criminology*, vol 19, no 3, pp 175-96.

Tappan, P.W. (1947) 'Who is the criminal?', *American Sociological Review*, vol 12, no 1, pp 96-102.

Taylor, M. (2005) 'Globalization and the internationalization of neoliberalism: the genesis and trajectory of societal restructuring in Chile', in S. Soederberg, G. Menz and P. Cerny (eds) *Internalizing globalization: The rise and the decline of national varieties of capitalism*, Basingstoke: Palgrave Macmillan, pp 183-99.

Thomas, B., Dorling, D. and Davey Smith, G. (2010) 'Inequalities in premature mortality in Britain: observational study from 1921 to 2007', *British Medical Journal*, vol 341, pp 3633-9.

Tifft, L.L. (1995) 'A social harms definition of crime', *Critical Criminologist*, vol 7, no 1, pp 9-13.

Tifft, L.L. and Sullivan, D. (2001) 'A needs-based, social harm definition of crime', in S. Henry and M.M. Lanier (eds) *What is crime? Controversies over the nature of crime and what to do about it*, Lanham, MD: Rowman & Littlefield, Chapter 14.

Toroyan, T. and Peden, M. (2007) *Youth and road safety*, Geneva: World Health Organization.

Townsend, P. (1993) *The international analysis of poverty*, Hemel Hempstead: Harvester Wheatsheaf.

UN Inter-agency Group for Child Mortality Estimation (2012) *Levels and trends in child mortality: Report 2012*, New York: UNICEF.

UNICEF (2001) *A league table of child deaths by injury in rich nations*, Innocenti Report Card 2, Florence: Innocenti, UNICEF.

UNODC (2013) *Global study on homicide 2013: Trends/contexts/data*, Vienna: United National Office on Drugs and Crime.

van Wanrooy, B. and Wilson, S. (2006) 'Convincing the toilers? Dilemmas of long working hours in Australia', *Work, Employment & Society*, vol 20, no 2, pp 349-68.

Veit-Wilson, J. (1999) 'Poverty and the adequacy of social security', in J. Ditch (ed) *Introduction to social security*, London: Routledge, pp 78-109.

Virtanen, M., Ferrie, J.E., Singh-Manoux, A., Shipley, M.J., Stansfeld, S.A., Marmot, M.G., Ahola, K., Vahtera, J. and Kivimäki, M. (2011) 'Long working hours and symptoms of anxiety and depression: a 5-year follow-up of the Whitehall II Study', *Psychological Medicine*, vol 18, pp 1-10.

Virtanen, M., Singh-Manoux, A., Ferrie, J.E., Gimeno, D., Marmot, M.G., Elovainio, M., Jokela, M., Vahtera, J. and Kivimäki, M. (2009) 'Long working hours and cognitive function: the Whitehall II Study', *American Journal of Epidemiology*, vol 169, no 5, pp 596-605.

Wagstaff, A.S. and Lie, J.-A.S. (2011) 'Shift and night work and long working hours: a systematic review of safety implications', *Scandinavian Journal of Work, Environment & Health*, pp 173-85.

Wang, Y.C., McPherson, K., Marsh, T., Gortmaker, S.L. and Brown, M. (2011) 'Health and economic burden of the projected obesity trends in the USA and the UK', *The Lancet*, vol 378, no 9793, pp 815-25.

Ward, T (2004) 'State harms', in P.Hillyard, C Pantazis, S Tombs, D Gordon (eds) *Beyond criminology: Taking harm seriously*, London: Pluto Press, pp 84-100.

Weiss, L. (2003) 'Introduction: Bringing domestic institutions back in', in L. Weiss (ed) *States in the global economy*, Cambridge: Cambridge University Press.

Wenger, C., Davies, R., Shahtamasebi, S. and Scott, A. (1996) 'Social isolation and loneliness in old age: review and model refinement', *Ageing & Society*, vol 6, pp 333-58.

WHO (World Health Organization) (2013) *Global status report on road safety 2013: Supporting a decade of action*, Geneva: WHO.

Wikeley, F., Bullock, K., Muschamp, Y. and Ridge, T. (2009) 'Educational relationships and their impact on poverty', *Education, Citizenship & Social Justice*, vol 5, no 2, pp 103-16.

Wilkins, L. (1982) 'Crime, quantification and the quality of life', in F. Elliston and N. Bowie (eds) *Ethics, public policy and criminal justice*, Cambridge, MA: Oelgeschlager, Gunn & Hain, pp 18-32.

Wilkinson, R. and Pickett, K. (2010) *The spirit level: Why equality is better for everyone*, Harmondsworth: Penguin.

Yar, M. (2012) 'Critical criminology, critical theory, and social harm', in S. Hall and S. Winlow (eds) *New directions in criminological theory*, Abingdon: Routledge, pp 52-65.

Index

H

Hall, P. 56
Hancke, B. 55
'harm,' defining 18–22, 23
harm indicators 73–8
harm reduction indicators 64–72
harm reduction regimes 53–72
harm-free society 33, 138, 151
harmful regime types continuum
  54–5, 64, 78–9, 103, 141
Harrington, J.M. 121
Harvey, D. 41, 46–7, 50, 51, 140
Hawkes, C. 97
Hay, C. 48
Hayek, F. 25
healthcare expenditure 67*t*, 93–4,
  96, 101, 146
Helliwell, J.F. 88
hidden harms 136
hierarchies of harm 23, 27–31
Hillyard, P. 4, 7, 8, 17, 18, 19, 23,
  36, 45
history of social harm concept 3–6,
  14–23
Holt-Lunstad, J. 130
homelessness 4, 41
homicide 73, 74, 81–7, 104
Hope, A. 5
House, J.S. 129
Howe, A. 5
Hughes, G. 5
human flourishing 18, 137, 138
human needs *see* needs-based
  definitions of social harm
human rights 15–16, 23
Hutton, W. 50

I

ideal types, use of 55–6, 66
identity 31, 83
illiteracy 29
impediments to successful human
  action 28, 73
imperialism 15, 16
imprisonment rates *see* penal
  systems
indicators of harm 73–8
indicators of harm reduction
  64–72
indifference, societal 8, 22, 144
individualistic approaches
  abstract individual 3, 138
  and criminology 4
  emphasis on individual agency
    2–3, 24–5, 40, 58
  homicide 82
  infant mortality 91

and needs-based definitions of
  social harm 138
suicide rates 89
individualistic societies
  alienation 38–9
  anomie 50
  autonomy/relational harms
    generally 145
  chaotic societies 104
  criminogenicity 58
  decommodification 133
  embedded liberalism vs
    neoliberalism 49
  and harm as personal failings 58
  social isolation 59, 132
inequality, social
  criminogenicity 58
  financial insecurity 117–18
  fragmented societies 104
  and greater incidence of harm 51
  as harm reduction indicator
    68–78
  homicide rates 83
  infant mortality 92–3
  obesity 99
  relative poverty 106–11
  road traffic injuries 100–1
  shame 83
  social isolation 130–1
  social solidarity 59, 144
  and state-sanctioned violence 43
inevitability (or otherwise) of harm
  8
infant mortality 74, 91–5, 104
injustice vs harm 19, 32
intentionality 8, 24–5, 81, 82
Ireland 65*t*, 70*t*, 142
irritants vs actual harm 24, 27
Italy 65*t*, 71*t*, 112, 127

J

Jackson, G. 55
Jacobs, D. 83
Jacobs, G. 101
Jäntti, M. 112
Japan 65*t*, 71*t*, 90, 145
Johnson, G. 88

K

Kauzlarich, D. 5
Kim, D.M. 98
Klein, N. 65
Kleppa, E. 121
Korea 65*t*, 71*t*, 83, 90, 97–8, 145
Kramer, R. 4, 16, 23

L

laissez-faire capitalism 1, 35, 139